CHILDREN OF GOD

A Memoir

By

Elizabeth Sutherland

Published November 2010 by
'For the Right Reasons Community Print'
60 Grant Street, Inverness, IV3 8BS
fortherightreasons@rocketmail.com
07717457247

ISBN 978-1-905787-55-5

Also by Elizabeth Sutherland:
The Black Isle, (nf) 1972; Lent Term (f) 1973; The Seer
of Kintail (f) 1974; Hannah Hereafter, (f) 1976; The Eye
of God, (f) 1977; The Prophecies of the Brahan Seer
(edit) (nf) 1977; The Weeping Tree, (f) 1980; Ravens and
Black Rain, (nf) 1985; The Gold Key and the Green Life
(edit)(nf) 1986; In search of the Picts, (nf) 1994; The
Pictish Trail, (nf) 1996; The Five Euphemias, (nf) 1997;
Lydia Wife of Hugh Miller of Cromarty, (b) 2002; The
Bird of Truth (f) 2006; Boniface, Bishops and Bonfires
(nf) 2010' Amendment of Life (f) 1010

CHILDREN OF GOD

A Memoir

Chapter One

Lies and Tears and Tea Parties

Memory and fact are only loosely related. The way Betty remembered it, she was flying. Flying was her favourite fantasy. Every night, 'Please God let me dream I'm flying,' was tagged on to her bedside prayers. It only worked once when she dreamed she was floating over the Hurlers, those little mounds that in her memory were like mountains. The first time she actually flew was out of the car window up into the dazzling white sky to land at the feet of an old gentleman who was looking down at her with kind and knowing eyes. She thought he might have been Father Christmas in ordinary clothes. Behind him she could see Annie dressed in her going-out clothes and laughing at her.

'But I did fly out of the window,' she told them all. 'I did,' she protested because by then everyone had given up arguing with her. Just like the time she saw the snake. They were driving to Shanwell in the old Standard B Nine on the twisty road through Glenfarg. The roof was down and the green sides of the valley rose steeply on either side of the road. She and Bunty sat on the back seat with Phillip and Charlotte, the two aged Sealyhams, between them. The snake was thick and grey, curled round a clump of bracken. 'I saw it. I know I saw it,' she screamed. After a while, the grown-ups gave up arguing.

What was the point? The more they argued the more she insisted. Thereafter, every time they drove past the place, someone always said 'that's-where-Betty-saw-the-snake'. Years later, indeed for the rest of her life, she could still see its coiled mass, grey and repulsive, just as she had seen it from the back of the car all those years ago. She could have taken you to the exact spot.

Was she lying then when she insisted that she had flown? At one level most certainly. It had been very stuffy in the car and she had tried to unwind the window. Instead she must have pushed down the door handle. It had opened and she had fallen out and concussed herself. The grown-ups knew that. When she saw the snake? Of course. Snakes so terrorised her imagination that one must have escaped into the real world.

There was a lot more to that flying experience that she only half remembered. It had not been a happy day. Tea parties with members of her father's congregation, usually elderly, were frequent and boring. This one had been better than most because other children were there and after tea they had gone into the garden to play and there had been a swing. Swinging was next best to flying. There were swings in the Park, hard to acquire because they were usually full of other children, not the sort to let you have a go. She would wait patiently for her turn but when it came someone else pushed in, so she kept on waiting or if Annie was getting bored moved off. There was a maypole too, a wondrous thing with ropes that you clung to, ran with and hung on. Some children swung round and round, flying with their feet high off the ground, but she never got the hang of it.

There was a swing at Shanwell, a sort of box thing you got into, but, somehow it was crooked and if you swung too high you crashed into the tree. The swing at the tea party had broken and she had fallen and hurt her knee. It had stung and she had cried for a long time which was why she was in the car with a bandaged knee. There had been a lot of other people in the back of the car and she had been pushed up against the door so she had opened the window and flown out.

Other children's nurseries were dominated by other people's nannies who were always stricter than Annie. 'We say please and thank you in our house,' they said reproachfully, or, 'we share our things in this nursery', while not so gently un-prising your fingers from a coveted toy. That was how she got Eddy. She fell in love with Eddy and no amount of un-prising would make her part with the smallish un-furry teddy bear that belonged to the family with the broken swing. 'Let her keep it,' a grown-up had told the prim Nanny when it was time to go home. 'It's the least we can do.'

Eddy was about eight inches tall. His squeak had long ago given up, but she could still feel it in his tummy, his seams showed through the worn fur and he had stitched eyes instead of glass ones and an optimistic stitched smile. He went everywhere with her, through childhood, boarding school, university and marriage. He was stolen on a troop-ship by an ex-Palestine policeman's child, which, she realised, was probably fair. She hoped that he was loved.

Eddy had fallen out of the car with her. Annie had found him in the gutter and he was the first thing she saw when she woke up from the concussion, lying stretched out on the sofa in the drawing-room, no, not quite the first thing. The first thing had been her father's eyes. Pure blue eyes, unflecked with grey and green as hers were, and brimming with tears. That had been more of a shock than flying. She had not realised that grown-ups could cry.

Grown ups, including her father, who cried were embarrassing. Like Mrs Burns. Mrs Burns was a devoted member of her father's congregation, a plump gushing sort of woman who said she adored children. 'Could the Rectory girls come to tea, please? I do so love little girls.' Arched eyebrows and coy smile. 'On their own?' They were deposited by Annie at Mrs Burns' front door at 4 pm precisely, to be called for at 5 30. It happened several times. They sat, all three of them, side by side on a sofa in a room that was full of cushions and lamps and photographs of a pretty little girl in a party frock who had once, incredibly, been Mrs Burns. They answered questions monosyllabically and munched through sandwiches, scones - she hated scones - and cakes, enormous fat chocolate éclairs bursting with cream. On the third visit Betty realised that Mrs Burns didn't mind if you ignored the sandwiches and skipped the scones, so, daringly, she reached out first for the chocolate-coated cake oozing cream. Bunty and Baby waited for a second, then, when the sky didn't fall in, followed her example. 'Oh dear,' said Mrs Burns all mock regret, 'no scones? What am I going to do with them?'

Bunty who always had the *bon mot*, still does, suggested, 'You could give them to the birds'.

'So I could,' said Mrs Burns. 'What a good idea, Barbara!' she gushed.

Betty ate two éclairs - and Mrs Burns never said a word. She didn't really want the second éclair but she was curious to see if she would be allowed to take it. One cake was the limit at home, but Mrs Burns didn't know how to say no.

That was another revelation. She had not yet come across a grown-up who couldn't say no.

After tea they all went out into the garden. It was a very hot day. They sat on deck chairs under a big shady umbrella. 'I want to be excused,' Baby said wriggling off her chair so Mrs Burns took her to the lavatory indoors.

'Let's hide,' she said to Bunty. There were lots of bushes and shrubs and flower beds and two rows of sweet peas. Bunty hid behind the tool shed. Betty pushed between the leafy branches of a huge rhododendron. There was a blackbird's nest within reach but to her disappointment it was empty. It was dark and dank and cool and she crouched down and waited. Presently Mrs Burns came back with Baby.

'They're hiding,' Baby explained.

'Let's find them,' Mrs Burns gushed clapping her hands together. 'Coo-ee!'

She did not answer. 'Coo-ee!' Mrs Burns shouted again while Baby flushed Bunty out from behind the tool-shed. 'Coo-ee, Elizabeth, where are you?' Mrs Burns sang. She always used their proper names.

Bunty found her at once but she lifted her finger to her lips and shook her head. Baby also found her but when Betty mouthed, 'shut up!' she just giggled and started rolling down the little slope that divided the wild part of the garden from the flower beds. 'Oh Florence. Be careful we'll spoil our pretty dress.'

7

'I hate it,' said Baby, rolling over and over in the grass.

Mrs Burns said placatingly, 'Who'll help me get some lemonade?'

Bunty said, 'I will,' and after a moment Baby got up and trotted after them.

They had forgotten about her. That was annoying. The longer she waited the more cross she became. When she heard them coming back, she peeped out between the leaves. Mrs Burns was carrying a tray with a jug full of home-made lemonade and four glasses. Bunty and Baby trotted happily beside her. The last thing she wanted was lemonade because she was still feeling sickish from the cakes, but she didn't like being ignored.

'Coo-ee!' she shouted encouragingly, but no one seemed to hear her. Mrs Burns poured the lemonade. 'These are my very best glasses,' she said. 'They came all the way from Venice. I only use them on very special occasions.'

'Is today a special occasion?' Baby asked curiously.

'It's always a special occasion when my girls come to tea.'

That finished her. She burst out of the bushes. 'I won!' she said. She was sparking with anger all over.

'Oh, there you are, dear,' said Mrs Burns triumphantly. 'We had forgotten all about you, hadn't we, girls?'

'You didn't win. I found you easily,' Bunty said contemptuously.

'So did I,' said Baby.

It could have been the start of one of their interminable arguments if Mrs Burns had not interrupted. 'You all won!' (How ridiculous, she thought.) 'Have some of my special lemonade in one of my special Venetian glasses, Elizabeth,' and then added with a laugh 'if you have room for it after all those éclairs.'

Electric with rage she took the proffered tumbler. It was a pretty glass, red and gold and it glittered in the sun. She lifted it to her lips and bit. It cracked satisfyingly under the teeth. She spat out a mouthful of glass and lemonade and blood on to the grass.

'Oh dear, oh dear, oh dear!' Mrs Burns was frantic. 'Are you all right, dear? Please, please don't swallow, just keep spitting. She started to thump her on the back. She spat again and again until her mouth was dry. Truth to tell she was a little scared.

'Sorry,' she muttered between spits.

'She did that on purpose,' Bunty accused. You could never get away with anything if Bunty was there.

'No I didn't,' she protested indignantly.

'You did, you did, you did!' Baby echoed.

She protested more loudly but they all knew what she had done.

Mrs Burns put the broken glass with the empty tumblers back on to the tray. In silence with her head bowed she lifted the tray and walked back to the house.

'She's crying,' Baby said accusingly. 'You made her cry.'

That was the first time she learned that you tended to hate the people you hurt.

There were no more tea parties at Mrs Burns.

But not all tea parties were disasters. Some were actually fun. Like the time Sister Grace and Sister Mabel Clare came to tea.

In her father's parish there was one Anglican convent. The nuns, or sisters as they were called, did social work in the slums of Dundee among the old and orphaned. When they were not working they lived a life of prayer and silence in their huge draughty Victorian house. Socialising was restricted to occasional visits to the Rectory because her father was their chaplain.

Sister Grace and Sister Mabel Clare wore the full habit, black in winter, grey in summer. It was still winter. How they got to the Rectory she never knew but presumably by tram. By 4 pm they had arrived and the three girls were sent down to the drawing room which sparkled as the open fire caught the shine of the big brass Indian tray, the silver cream jug, sugar and slop bowls, the blue Wedgwood teacups rimmed with gold. Plates, snowy napkins and little knives with mother-of-pearl handles were set on occasional tables and there were butter-balls, which Baby had helped Hannah to make, and home-made strawberry jam. A cake stand held the usual array of Mina's scones, pancakes and a Victoria sponge.

After the introductions and comments on the weather, the bowls of blue hyacinths and the view (it was a lovely view across the River Tay) there was silence. Father was not there to tease them and mother was, on this occasion, as shy as the two black-clad sisters, which paralysed the children. Hannah came in with the silver tea-pot and hot water jug. The silence stretched between them like the two old dogs who had settled to snooze on the hearth-rug in front of the blazing fire. Everyone sat on the edges of their chairs and smiled politely.

Suddenly Bunty could bear it no longer. 'Give that girl a cup of tea,' she told her mother in a loud voice indicating the tall aristocratic Sister Grace.

Shocked silence. Girl she was not. Then suddenly Sister Grace hooted with laughter. Baby got up and turned a somersault (her latest achievement), Betty handed rounded the scones and everyone was talking and laughing at once.

When their father returned, they were all down on the floor playing *Racing Demon*. Sister Mabel Clare beat Bunty, who was the acknowledged champion. 'I'm sure she cheated,' Bunt said admiringly after they had gone.

Afterwards Father laughed too till the tears rolled down his cheeks. Happy tears.

There were so many different kinds of tears and she had cried them all, angry tears, sad tears, sore tears, baby tears, patriotic tears like when the King broadcast on the wireless at Christmas and you all stood up for the National Anthem. Father did not even try to hide those tears. The worst sort were false tears.

When she was five she had been sent down the hill to a small private school in the top flat of a tenement building. It had been recommended by the people who lived next door to the Rectory, two brothers and a sister who were all much older than she was, at least eight or nine. 'They can all walk down together,' Mrs Morgan suggested. Betty wasn't there long, perhaps only a few weeks. She had thought it rather odd at the time, having to stand on the table and take her knickers off.

'It's what cry-babies have to do,' the next-door neighbour girl who was called Joan explained, but she wouldn't have cried if they had not made her take her knickers off. She hadn't cried even when the teacher rapped her knuckles with a ruler for making her letters crooked, well, maybe a few tears, because it was sore, but not proper boo-hoo crying.

She never went back and that was a relief. Although she had quite liked one of the next-door neighbour boys who was called Gemmel, she was bewildered by school, the weird customs and the difficult conversations.

A few weeks later a governess called Miss Taylor arrived. The nursery was transformed into a schoolroom, the big white table was moved from the window recess to the middle of the room and there were notebooks and spelling books and pencils and rubbers neatly arranged in two separate piles, one for her and one for Bunty. The clothes that always aired on the tall brass-rimmed fireguard had been whipped away, and, instead of Annie sitting on a basket chair toasting her knees and darning socks, Miss Taylor sat primly at the head of the nursery table. Betty sat on one side with her back to the fire and Bunty sat opposite. Baby had a little table in the window recess and a whole box full of crayons to keep her quiet. (It didn't really work so Annie was summoned to remove her a few minutes later. She can't have been much over two.)

Miss Taylor didn't last any longer than the school. 'They are the rudest children I've even known,' she said to Mother, her hairpins flying, her glasses glinting behind dry and angry eyes. She and Bunty had hung their heads in shame. Rudeness was almost unforgivable. It involved God.

Her rudeness was not in dispute. She was not exactly sure why she had been behaved so badly but she knew that Miss Taylor was the silliest person she had ever met. It was another discovery on a par with grown-ups weeping, that grown-ups could be silly. 'Don't be silly,' Mother would say to her in a dismissive sort of way when she had been arguing, playing the fool or ragging with her sisters. Or, as Auntie Meg would put it, 'You're such a gowk.' Gowk meant cuckoo. To call Miss Taylor a gowk was to insult cuckoos. She was far sillier than that.

It was something to do with her hair. She dropped hairpins when she was agitated. They flew on to the table, scattered on the carpet and stuck out of her untidy wispy bun.

'Why does your hair always look like a bird's nest?' she had asked. It had not been a pleasant question. She could hear with amazement the scorn in her voice. Untidy hair was not approved of in the Rectory. Annie anchored hers with slides and kirby grips.

'Oh dear,' said Miss Taylor in a baby voice. 'I'm a naughty girl then, am I?'

Bunty joined in, 'You're not a girl,' she said equally scornfully. She was still touchy about Sister Grace.

'And you are a very rude child.' Miss Mitchell retorted in a wobbly grown-up voice. 'You are both rude children. I am doing my best to teach you. You will both go and stand in the corner.'

They had looked at each other in horror. Standing in the corner was for babies. Not even Baby at her naughtiest was ever stood in the corner. Neither of them had moved. 'Do as I tell you at once,' she blustered.

It occurred to both sisters at the same time that this was an order they could disobey which was another revelation. It had never occurred to either of them that

13

you did not always have to do as you were told. So they sat still. Besides, there were no corners in the nursery unless you squeezed in behind the toy chest.

Then the horror started. Miss Taylor began to cry, but they weren't real tears nor was it proper crying. 'Maybe I'm the naughty girl. Is that it? Boo-hoo. Perhaps you want me to stand in the corner?'

When neither child spoke, she crossed the room, hairpins flying, to the far end of the large sunny nursery beside the white painted chest of drawers that kept their combinations and stays, put her hands to her eyes and continued noisily and falsely to cry.

Annie came in at that moment with a tray of milk and biscuits and a cup of coffee for Miss Taylor. She looked questionably at each of them as she put it down on the table. 'I've been naughty so they put me in the corner,' Miss Taylor explained in a little girl voice. There was not a trace of tears on her face.

Annie said nothing but her eyes raked the two children mercilessly. Betty knew that would mean a row later. It was an almighty row and Father was told. Sorry tears followed and early bed. They both learned there was just so far you could go when it came to disobeying a grown-up.

Miss Taylor did not return. As it was almost time for the summer holidays there were no more lessons for a while.

Instead there was Shanwell. Her parents drove up to Father's home in Orkney leaving the children with Auntie Meg and there were tea parties or picnics nearly every day.

Aged cousins in wide-brimmed straw hats in ancient motors rolled over the gravel, neighbours with walking sticks and dogs strode across the lawn, friends from the village three miles away, sometimes with grandchildren or nieces and nephews, turned up on bicycles and sat in canvas chairs round a wicker table to indulge in scones and gingerbread and fairy cakes baked by Annie-the-cook and scattered with hundreds and thousands. The children lounged on the lawn on tartan rugs under a hot sun while the grown-ups sipped china tea and talked.

Provided they said 'how do you do' politely, did not interrupt, and drank their milk, nobody minded if they sloped off to hit a croquet ball across the grass or swing in the hammock that was slung between two aged elms at the far end of the lawn, or play hide-and-seek in the shrubbery. These tea parties would have been almost fun but for the wasps. Squadrons of them. Auntie Meg who had spent some years in India pooh-poohed their frantic swatting. 'Leave them alone. They won't sting you if you sit perfectly still.'

Not true She had once sat perfectly still at the nursery table joining up dots in her fun book and she had not realised that a wasp was crawling up her leg until it stung her under the knee. When she tried to tell Auntie Meg, she had said, 'Don't be a perfect fool! Of course you frightened it.'

But wasps are sneaky creatures. One crawled inside a jammy scone and Auntie Meg bit it in two. Fortunately the stingy end was left in the scone, but the head end was still wriggling in her mouth before she spat it out into her napkin. She did a lot of flapping and dancing around that day too, and the awful thing was Betty had wanted to laugh. It was agony holding in the laugh because Auntie Meg did not think it the least bit funny.

When no one came to tea they went out to tea. Every summer Auntie Meg drove them to Cousin Ella who lived in a castle, wore enormous hats and had a Japanese garden looked after by a Japanese gardener. After a meal of tiny cucumber sandwiches and dark fruit cake in the lofty dining room where they sat on tall chairs with tapestry seats which had been covered with dust cloths for the children, they were taken by Cousin Ella's companion to see Cousin Ella's famous dolls' house, a truly magical creation which they were not allowed to touch, they were at last sent out to play in the garden. It was her dearest wish to find the gardener, who, Auntie Meg had told them somewhat acidly, sang when he was miserable which was all the time. They found the garden with its little humpy bridges and searched the shrubbery but to her disappointment there was no sight or sound of the Japanese gardener.

That was the summer of the silver Jubilee when the old king and Queen Mary who looked exactly like Cousin Ella and who, it was rumoured, was her personal friend because they shared a rivalous interest in dolls' houses, celebrated their twenty-five years on the throne with bonfires on all the surrounding hilltops.

That night, that glorious night, she had been allowed, for the first time, to stay up for dinner in order to see the bonfires. Dinner at Shanwell meant changing into a party frock. Mother and Auntie Meg wore long gowns and father exchanged his holiday plus-fours for his black clerical suit. The dining room table glittered with candles. Father carved her favourite roast chicken and gave her the

16

wish-bone with one of Annie-the-Cook's big crispy roast potatoes; for pudding she ate the first of the strawberries with lots of sugar and cream. Her excitement was intense. She talked too much but for once the grown-ups were indulgent and laughed and listened. She even tried a mouthful of wine but it was horrible.

It seemed a long time to wait for it to get dark, but, at last it was time to get into the car to drive to a good place to see all the hills at once. There was quite an argument among the grow-ups about that, but, by this time, she was getting really sleepy and had to concentrate to keep awake. She must have dozed off because next thing she knew she was clambering out of the car, and, there, all round on the tops of Ochils, the Cleish Hills, Benarty and the Lomonds, were bonfires, like a necklace of lights.

That was also the year of the snake. It had all started at the dentist. Her new teeth were too big for her jaw so she had to have four of them removed. She sat on the dentist's chair and a football was put over her nose which smelt evil. Then she had a dream, a sad dream about a doll which had walked up to the shop window and pressed its button nose against the pane and screamed. Then she realised that it was she who was screaming and there was a lot of blood and the dentist was telling her it was all over and she had been such a good girl. The screaming turned to sobs and the sobs to hiccups by the time she got home. She was allowed to lie on the sofa in the drawing-room with one of mother's silk scarves over her mouth and father came out of his study and sat beside her and read her the story of the cocky little mongoose called Rikki Tikki Tavi and his battles with the two terrible cobras, Nag and Nagina. Father was a good reader and when he hissed in snake-like fashion, 'I am Nag....Look and be afraid,' she was terrified. Thereafter she could not even look at the big red book of *Animal Stories* by Rudyard Kipling without fear. She saw snakes everywhere, behind closed doors, in the potting shed, at the bottom of her bed in the middle of the night. In Glenfarg. She was to remain terrified of snakes, until, as an adult in Africa, she nearly trod on a green mamba and realised that it was equally scared of her.

So was it a lie, the coiled grey snake in Glenfarg? If she could still see it in her imagination, believed she saw it, insisted that she had seen it but hadn't, could you call it a lie? Not like a real lie. Not like that time in Elie.

Once, when Auntie Meg was too ill to have the children at Shanwell while their parents were in Orkney, Annie took the three of them on holiday to the sea-side in Elie. They shared two rooms in a very strict boarding house that looked out over a narrow street. No sand shoes allowed indoors, no wet bathing suits to be hung on the window sills, no staying out after 10 pm. Not that any of this mattered to them. They were down on the beach from 9am till 5pm and tucked up in bed with stories read by 8 pm.

It was a wondrous time. Sand castles of stupendous proportions were built with little slides and tunnels for golf balls. Forts and moats and dams bravely withstood the incoming tide. Bathing was twice a day, wet or dry, with a little hut to change in and pony rides cost 6d a time. Once, just once, she had been allowed to ride Lazy Mary back to the stables free where the ponies stayed overnight. It was the only time Lazy Mary ever cantered. Mostly she strolled a little way into the waves and

18

refused to budge in spite of coaxing with sugar lumps and timid kicks on the flanks until shouted at by her owner, a fiery Irish adolescent with spots and frizzy red hair. But she loved Lazy Mary and all her saved pocket money went on rides.

Meanwhile Annie had made friends with another Nanny, a chatty uniformed Glaswegian in charge of a family of three children, two boys and a girl, called Duncan who always seemed to have enough money to buy ice cream cones, new buckets and beach balls, and to have pony rides whenever they liked. Annie said with awe that they were very rich. 'Well-off, you mean,' Betty corrected, sorry, 'badly-off' people - could be rich in other ways. 'Are we well-off or rich then,' she had asked but mother had not answered. It was bad manners to talk about wealth.

One wet day, Nanny Duncan asked Annie and the three girls to tea. They changed into clean cotton dresses and trooped down the esplanade to the Grand Hotel where the Duncans had a suite of rooms overlooking the beach. It was obvious by then they were extremely well-off.

'Afternoon tea' was brought up by a uniformed maid at 3 pm and there were things to eat called cream horns and her absolute favourite cream cookies dusted with icing sugar and filled with a sweet sticky substance that called itself cream but tasted much nicer. They played snakes and ladders and ludo and then the girl, May, who was about her age, took her into her bedroom to put her dolls to bed. She was rather bossy. 'I'm the Nanny' she said.'You can be the maid. You have to call me ma'am,' only she pronounced it 'mum', and sent her to the wardrobe to fetch the dolls' nighties.

There were two drawers in the wardrobe under the hanging space. She opened the wrong one. It was full of chocolate bars. She stared at them in astonishment. They were wrapped in gold foil covered by yellow and brown paper and they were all labelled Duncan. 'Not that drawer, you stupid girl,' May said in her nanny voice, 'the other one.'

'Sorry mum,' she said contritely but all she could think of was the chocolate in the drawer. 'Did your father make all that chocolate?' she asked.

'Of course not, stupid. He has a factory. Let's get on with the game.'

The thought of the chocolate dominated her mind. She could almost taste it. Surely they wouldn't miss one out of so many? Next time she was sent to fetch more clothes for the dolls she secretly withdrew a bar and slipped it into the pocket of her cotton dress.

When she got home she hid it under her pillow. After Annie had read to them and hugged them goodnight, she waited till Bunty was asleep and took out the bar. Although the thin curtains had been drawn it was light enough to unwrap the gold paper and bite off a succulent chunk. Horror of horrors. It was full of nuts. She hated chocolate with nuts in it so she spat it out into her handkerchief. Worse was to follow. Annie came back. 'Are you eating something?'

'No,' she lied, her mouth smeared with the stuff and her pillow covered with brown streaks. Then when Annie asked her outright if she had been eating chocolate she told another lie. 'May gave it to me,' she said earnestly. 'You should have shared it with your sisters,' Annie said.

'They can have it.' she said generously pulling out the remains of the bar.

So nothing more was said, but that was two lies in as many minutes. God would not be pleased.

Chapter Two

God, Elephants and the Sweetie Jar

There were nine people living in the Rectory. Mother and Father downstairs, the three children and Annie in the nursery, Hannah, the house parlour-maid and Mina the cook in the kitchen made eight, and God, unseen maybe, but none the less real for that. The trouble with God was that you never knew where he might be. He had, as Annie would say 'eyes in the back of his head,' which Annie hadn't, or so she insisted, when she lost a sock in the laundry or Baby dropped toothpaste on the carpet. 'Do you think I've got eyes at the back of my head?' she would say crossly.

God had eyes everywhere. It said so in the Bible. This meant you might well be able to 'get away with murder', according to Annie, as far as the grown-ups were concerned but you could never ever escape the eye of God. Fortunately God didn't tell tales. On the other hand it was down to you to own up. If you did, God forgave you, but if you didn't, God would suffer. Sometimes she suffered too. Suffering meant early bed and no story. On the whole it was better to own up and get it over and done with. 'Getting away with it,' was never much fun. Like that time with the chocolate.

It never occurred to her that God might not be real. Although unseen, there was plenty of evidence of his existence. God came in three parts like a clover-leaf.

God-the-Father was not unlike her own father when he dressed up in his chasuble and stood at the glittering cathedral altar surrounded by servers with bells and incense. God-the-Father expected you to go to church, expected you to be good, and expected you to love him. And she did. Well…sort of. God-the-Father was a bit intimidating. He might ask you to do difficult things like Abraham with Isaac, or Noah and the Ark. Tests. She was quite good at tests in lessons but she knew these were not the sort of tests God would set. His tests were far more difficult, like the time she found sixpence in the street and hastily spent it on a tracing book, a sherbet sucker and sugar cigarettes before she could be told to put it in the church collection. Afterwards Father explained to her .that this was why everyone said *lead us not into temptation* in the Lord's Prayer. It was not that she had done anything badly wrong on that occasion but that she could have done something better.

God-the-Son, called Lord Jesus, looked like the kind man in the long white gown with a sheep slung over his shoulder holding the hand of a little boy or it might have been a girl because he or she was wearing a long white nightie too. The picture was in her hymn-book opposite *Loving Shepherd of thy sheep* which was her almost-favourite hymn. He was the one who got really hurt when you were naughty. You had to try not to do anything to hurt him. Bad people put him on the cross to die, but those bad people were just like us. If she was naughty, he hung on the cross all over again. He also expected you to love him, and she did. 'I love you, Lord Jesus,' she said every night at the end of her prayers.

The third part of God was called the Holy Ghost. He didn't look like a ghost though. If you could have seen him he would have looked like a sparkly white pigeon. He was that part of God that knew all about her and could hear every thought in her head. He was the one who made her feel miserable when she had been naughty. The Holy Ghost came to live inside babies when they were baptised (Bunty thought it was capsized) and became children of God. So God was really everywhere, inside and out, in the Church, in the stars, in the street, in the heart and in the head. 'Three persons in one God,' her father told her. It was easier to understand if you thought of the clover leaf, or, if you came to think of it, a tricycle.

God was not the only other person in the family. There were also guardian angels. If everyone had a guardian angel, as father said, that made quite a crowd. She had once tried to count them. Did guardian angels look like the people they guarded? Did they start off as cherubs and end up with long grey hair like Auntie Meg, or maybe their wings went grey. Did they die when you died or did they go on to look after someone else? Maybe, after you died and you were good, you could become an angel. Angels could fly. It said so in her most favourite hymn. *Oh that I had wings of angels/ here to spread and heavenward fly/ I would seek the gates of heaven /far above the starry sky.'* She would like to become an angel.

Having God and all those angels around all the time was scary if you thought too much about it.

The part of God she liked best was Baby Jesus. Above her bed she had a picture of him in the arms of his mother, Mary, standing in a garden of lilies. He was so sweet, holding out his own little arms and smiling. He was the one she thought of every night as she knelt by her bed and father or mother or Annie heard her prayers. He was the one she thanked for her life, her home and her happy day, the one she asked to bless her family, her friends and the dogs. He was the one to whom she said sorry every night.

One of the best things about Baby Jesus was his birthday. 'How can he be born again every Christmas?' she once asked her mother. 'Born again in your heart, darling,' she said as if that explained everything. She realised dimly that there were some things no one could explain and that it didn't much matter. Christmas was one of them.

Christmas always started weeks before on the night they wrote their letters to Father Christmas. They wrote them in their best writing and mother threw them into the drawing-room fire, one at a time, at the top nearest to the chimney and usually they shot up and out of sight, almost as if an invisible hand had come down and snatched them. Sometimes if you folded yours too tightly it sank into the flames and had to be retrieved with the tongs. Once hers got very badly singed. 'Will Father Christmas still be able to read it?' she asked anxiously. 'Of course,' said her mother without thinking.

'Please can I have a baby doll,' she had written that year. Next year it was a dolls' cradle, then a dolls' pram, then a dolls' house, a scooter, a bicycle… You only ever asked for one thing and it was always better than you imagined it would be. The baby doll was called Elspeth and mother gave her a long white lawn dress that all three girls had worn when they were tiny. She was as big as a real baby. Bunty's one was a little smaller called Mary Rose and Baby was given Sailor Boy. She didn't like girl dolls. The cradle was made of blue wicker by the Blind Institute and big enough for a real baby. The pram was a dark creamy colour with a proper hood, a waterproof cover, a brake and a seat in the middle of the bottom you could take out so that a real baby could sit in it. Taking Elspeth for a walk in the park made her feel grown-up and proud. Bunty's pram was marginally smaller and navy blue and Baby got a kiddy car.

That year, after the horrid school, she was dawdling in the park behind her mother. Baby was in the push-chair and Bunty holding on to the pram handle. She was in a bad mood so she asked the unthinkable question because it had been lying uneasily in the bottom of her mind for a long time. 'Father Christmas isn't a real person is he? Joan said he's just you and daddy.'

Mother should have said 'Of course he's real'. Instead she waited until Bunty had run on ahead then went into a long explanation of how God wanted to give children presents on his Son's birthday so he did it through Santa Claus who had once been Saint Nicholas, a real king, but was now in heaven so he had to do it through mummies and daddies.'

She was furious. 'You shouldn't have told me,' she stormed. 'Now you've spoiled it all.'

'Then don't spoil it for Bunty,' was all Mother said. Of course she told Bunty, but Bunty didn't believe her, and when Christmas came around everything was just the same as it had always been. She wrote her letter as usual. She heard the carol singers several streets away singing

Hark the herald Angels Sing and she finished her needle book for Mother and her pen-wiper for Father.

She spent hours trying to write a Christmas carol to put in her home-made cards. Rhyming was the trouble. 'Manger' went with 'danger'. 'God' was difficult. You couldn't do much with 'sod' and 'clod'. 'Night' and 'day' were both good for they gave you a wide choice. After a lot of crossings-out she came up with: 'In that little stable gay/ A little head lay on the hay/ Jesus whom we all adore/ Lying on a bed of straw.' She was not too happy about 'straw' and 'adore' because they didn't look right on paper. And could you really call a stable 'gay'? She tried again: 'Christmas is a time of joy/ All because a little boy,/ He whom all the angels love,/ Came to us from heaven above.' Much better. Painstakingly she copied it out on three cards, one for mother and father, one for Suthy and one for Auntie Meg. All of them had a drawing of the manger and a baby – she was good at doing babies in profile - with yellow sparks of light coming from his head. She was quite pleased with them.

In the week before Christmas right up to Christmas morning, the postie delivered a lot of parcels because between them they had nine godparents. They were all kept on top of the bookcase that lined one wall of father's study. If you stood on a chair you could reach them and shake them. You always knew the ones which were chocolates because they rattled. 'Only chocolates' she would say sadly to Bunty. Chocolates, jigsaws, and, worst of all, handkerchiefs were disappointing. Books were best unless it was something really special like the cuddly puppies in a puppy basket that Baby was given by her godmother, or the three little pigs that played instruments when you wound them up which was Bunty's favourite of all time, or the white pompadour wig for dressing up as a princess that Annie gave her.

Otherwise her best presents were books. Each year for four years running she was given one of Mrs Molesworth's novels all in the same matching blue binding. *The Tapestry Room* was her favourite. Auntie Meg always gave marvellous presents. Sheets and blankets and a miniature eiderdown for the cradle, another year a girl doll with straight brown hair like her own and painted brown eyes wearing a red taffeta frock, called Christina, and once, unforgettably, a toy typewriter that sometimes really worked to print out her poems. That became her absolute favourite.

One Christmas morning after she had felt the familiar thrilling crackle of paper and felt the exciting little lumps inside one of father's walking socks, she saw in the dim light of dawn beside her bed the gleaming handle-bar of a small bicycle, a fairy cycle, to give it its proper name. Bunty got a tricycle that year and Baby, a smaller version, that could be ridden indoors and on which she careered up and down the upstairs passage to the danger of all.

Christmas morning meant postie with lots more cards and sometimes postal orders for half a crown, and, of course, Matins. The cathedral was full of smiling people, and, instead of hymns, some of which could be very long and boring with unfamiliar tunes, there were carols which everyone knew. The mad lady who sat two rows behind them and vigorously shook her handbag full of pennies whenever Father Donaldson or Father Hemming preached sat quietly because today it was the bishop. As

27

it was a special occasion they were allowed to eat the big white peppermint sweet that the verger surreptitiously handed out to children to suck during the sermon. It was so big it lasted the full twenty minutes.

Then there was Christmas lunch and Auntie Meg was always there with her two dogs. Christmas pudding was stuffed full of tiny parcels wrapped in greaseproof paper containing silver horseshoes, rings and three-penny bits. No-one liked to get the thimble because that meant you would be an old maid. Mina the cook learned to leave out the thimble because it caused arguments, sometimes even tears. One year she put in nothing but threepenny bits.

Opening the presents came after lunch, one at a time and no snatching. Mother wrote down everything and Auntie Meg smoothed out the brown wrapping paper and folded it for next year.

Then they all went for a walk in the park and she was allowed to take her new cycle. Father held on to the seat as she wobbled along the path. Bunty peddled ahead showing off her new tricycle and mother helped Baby while Auntie Meg coped with the dogs.

'I can do it!' she told her father after a while. 'I can manage by myself!' so off she peddled down the long grassy slope of the park wobbling, proud and terrified, faster and faster. Steering was still a problem. Stopping impossible. Like a magnet she was drawn to the only other family on the path at the bottom of the hill. 'Watch out!' someone shouted indignantly. 'Put on your brakes!' her father advised from the top of the slope. Too late.

The other family tried to leap out of the way as she ploughed a furrow right through them and fell off at their feet. They were none too pleased, but no one was hurt, only her pride. Bunty looked smug. 'It's not funny!' Betty protested glaring at her family. 'Of course it isn't,' father agreed seriously. 'You might have hurt someone.' He was trying not to laugh too.

As she was in a huff, she refused to let anyone help her so she pushed the fairy cycle all the way to the pond. The ducks clamoured for crusts as usual and the swans were there today. They flapped their wings and flew at the dogs. Auntie Meg was cross. 'Don't you realise swans can break a dog's back with their necks?' she said, hastily leashing her spaniels. So Betty forgot about the crash and allowed father to hold her saddle all the way home.

After tea with Christmas cake they lit the Christmas tree. It dominated a corner of the drawing-room and had red wax candles with barley sugar stems clipped on to the ends of the branches. It looked and smelled wonderful but Father was always anxious about those candles in case of fire and had the children blow them out before he disappeared back to the cathedral. Then they played games. *Old Maid* was a bit of a problem for the loser, so it was solved by sugar lumps. *Happy Families* caused arguments. You had to say, 'Please may I have Mrs Bun the Baker's Wife,' and 'Thank-you,' if you got it, otherwise it didn't count. It meant shouting it loudly several times otherwise you might not be heard.

But Christmas was not over yet. During the next few days there was the Carol Service at the Crib, the Sunday School Party and best of all the Nativity Play. The angels were dressed in white nighties and crepe paper wings with tinsel tied round their hair, shepherds in dressing gowns with tea towels on their heads, Mary in a blue blanket with her baby doll. 'Why can't I go to Sunday

School?' she whined every year. Sunday School had picnics and parties and plays. She never had a satisfactory answer.

The nearest she got to Sunday School was in Lent. Father had a children's service on Fridays evenings at 6 pm in the cathedral. He told good stories about a boy called Bill, and, joy of joy, the children were each given a little blue cardboard folder with six spaces and every week they got a new stamp with a picture of Jesus on it to stick in the folder. The aim was to get six stamps. One Friday she had a cold and wasn't allowed to go so she got no stamp. She cried herself sick, but rules were rules.

Father Donaldson celebrated a children's Mass in one of the cathedral's daughter churches on Saturday mornings in Lent, so mother took them to that. They had special little booklets with pictures in them instead of prayer-books and the writing was easy to read. Father Donaldson was strange, though. One moment he would be at the altar and then suddenly he would be kneeling at your side in all his robes smelling of incense and still praying very loudly. Children were allowed to help him and he might call anyone up out of the congregation at any time. She lived in constant anticipation that he might call her, but, to her disappointment, he never did.

Lent meant no sweets. That was hard. Usually they were allowed two a day after lunch and to spend their Saturday pocket money on sweets but in Lent, rules were rules. Gerald told them that he was allowed sweets on Sundays. 'Dad says Sundays aren't Lent,' he pronounced in a lordly fashion, but even though his father was a priest like theirs, they didn't believe him. They thought he was cheating.

During Lent they hardly saw their father and in Holy Week not at all. An atmosphere of gloom hung over the household as if the blinds were drawn. Good Fridays were painful days culminating in the *Three Hours* service from noon till 3 pm in the cathedral. Mostly it was taken by a visiting priest while father preached elsewhere. He was 'in great demand for the Three Hours Devotion', mother told her, so she told Gerald in her most squashing voice, and, for once, he was silent. One year when father was in his own cathedral, mother told them he had to preach seven sermons – seven sermons?

'Do we have to go?' she asked mother who thought she could have put the question a better way. 'Do you want to go?' she asked sternly so what else could she say but 'yes' in a very small voice. 'We'll think about it,' her mother told her.

It was decided that they were old enough to go to the last hour. That meant they would only hear two of the sermons. The cathedral was shrouded in its purple Lenten drapery, no flowers, no organ, no choir, only father in his black cassock. They were singing one of her favourite hymns, *When I survey the wondrous cross*, as they slipped in to the half-full, strangely sombre building. The singing was led by Father Hemming in his cassock sitting in the front pew. With no organ she could hear herself sing. She thought she sounded rather nice.

Several other children had come in for the last hour too, so they sang *There is a green hill far away without a city wall*. Why, she always wondered, should a hill have a wall at all? Perhaps most hills had walls in Palestine. She tried to picture it in her head.

As it was such a lovely day Mother had arranged a treat for after the service; a picnic at Kinnaird. Father would be very tired so they were warned not to argue and not to forget it was still Good Friday. They promised. But father did not seem tired. They ran ahead of him and mother among the daffodils and after a while they forgot it was Good Friday and screamed with laughter as they played *Tig* and *Tom Tiddlers Ground* in the pale spring sunshine. Father was still wearing his black gaiters and frock coat but he laughed and teased them and hungrily ate most of the sandwiches.

Then on Easter Day there were Easter Eggs. The cardboard ones that opened out and had little presents inside were best. They ate boiled eggs for breakfast and the cathedral was full of flowers and light and music. In the afternoon they hunted for eggs in the garden, each one boiled hard and exquisitely painted with their names on them. Betty's one had a little cat, Bunty had Barbar the Elephant on hers and Baby had two little puppies. They were far too good to eat so they sat on the nursery mantelpiece, and, after a while, of course, Annie quietly removed them. Suthy had made them and Annie had hidden them in the garden while they were all at the cathedral.

Suthy was one of the best things that ever happened to her. After the disaster of school, then Miss Taylor, a new governess was imperative. Helen Sutherland was recommended for the job, interviewed and stayed. She lived with her father, a Professor Emeritus of Natural History at St Andrews University, on the other side of the Tay at Newport, and crossed the river every morning on the 8am ferry. Sometimes, but not often, she brought her little dog, an odious wire-haired terrier who bit and who had to be kept apart from Phillip and Charlotte in their playroom where he savaged their toys - a good incentive for keeping the room tidy, as Annie told them tartly.

Suthy was tall and thin with long dark wavy hair caught up in a neat bun, dark brown eyes and a large nose and mouth with a lot of very strong, sticky-out teeth. She smiled easily but she could be strict. You would never think of standing Suthy in a corner. She was not a trained teacher but she followed the PNEU (Parents National Educational Union) curriculum, devised for home tutoring. It included boring subjects such as Citizenship. *Plutarch's Lives* were incomprehensible to her as well as tedious. The course did not seem to include much grammar or any Latin and French but it devoted a lot of time to the old gods. *Tales of Greece and Rome* collected by Andrew Lang became her favourite of all favourite books.

Suthy told them stories. She wrote them down in a red notebook so Betty had to have a red notebook too where she painstakingly wrote down long involved stories about dragons and witches and fairies. She always started them with 'Once upon a time and by that I mean a very long time ago...' because that's how Suthy started her stories. She was allowed to write her stories while Suthy concentrated on teaching Bunty and Gerald and Baby and Michael who sat at little green desks in the window alcove

Suthy had inherited from her father his love and knowledge of nature. Every morning at 10.30 they went for a nature walk in the park. They found acorns in egg-cups and grew them into tiny trees, sycamore wings that

33

sprouted long curving shoots, chestnuts and made them into dolls' house furniture with match sticks, fished for tadpoles in the pond with little green nets stuck on to the end of long thin canes. They searched for wild flowers, pressed them in blotting paper under a pile of heavy volumes and then pasted them into scrap-books with the date and place they had found them. She learned all about trees, dried their leaves in autumn, then beat them with a hair brush until they became delicate skeletons like little pieces of fine lace.

But Suthy's favourite in all nature was birds. They watched birds, they fed birds and she learned their names and their habits. Once there was a waxwing in the garden and Suthy was so excited that they spent most of the afternoon with their noses pressed to the window, watching. It was Suthy's idea that she should collect birds' eggs, one only from a nest, though. She showed her how to make a tiny hole in the top and bottom of the egg with a needle then blow the insides out. She never managed to do this herself but Annie could. Annie became as interested in finding nests as she did and so did all the family.

She took her *Observers Book of Wild Birds* everywhere she went. (Once, though, she left it outside all night and it had rained so it never looked quite the same again.) She layered a shoebox in cotton wool and soon her collection numbered a blackbird's blue oval scribbled all over in pale brown which she found in the beech hedge in Dundee. The crow's egg was a bit of a cheat. She had found a perfect half lying among other bits of shell under the rookery in the park. You couldn't tell unless you turned it over. Her first real success was the yellow

34

hammer's nest found in a whin bush at Shanwell. Suthy was excited when she told her about it. 'Did you hear what it sang?' Betty shook her head. She had had eyes only for the five little pale pink eggs covered with purply squiggles and her thoughts were on how to push her hand through all those prickles. 'Listen next time,' Suthy told her, 'and you'll hear it singing "Deil-deil-deil-tak-ye".' All her good finds were at Shanwell and best of all was down by the Spout in between the mossy boulders of an old wall, where she spotted a wren's perfect ball of a nest with five tiny little eggs.

Gerald was very scornful of her collection. 'Do you realise that each of those eggs represents a living bird? It's stealing.' He was quoting his mother, a strange lady with purple finger nails who had told him it was cruel. She wondered about this.

'As long as you take only one and don't disturb the nest any more than you have to,' Suthy said. Her father, the professor, had an enormous collection in a special bookcase with little drawers. He sent her a tern's egg which he had found on the beach in St Andrews and took a great, if distant, interest in her collection.

She supposed she learned something from the eggs and the shapes and places of the nests but she always whispered, 'sorry', when she stole the precious egg and felt increasingly guilty. After a while the egg collection sat on the top shelf of the nursery and gathered dust.

Gerald arrived every morning at nine o'clock from the neighbouring parish driven by his saturnine father of whom she was deeply afraid. That Gerald was afraid of him too she did not realise until the episode of the matches. 'Look what I've got!' he boasted one morning in the nursery before Suthy arrived. She was allowed a quick glimpse of a box of Swan Vestas which he had concealed in the pockets of his shorts. Matches were forbidden. Heinrich Hoffmann's *Dreadful Story about Harriet and the Matc*hes about the little girl who *would not take Mamma's advice and lit a match, it was so nice,* was one of their least favourite bedtime stories.

'Where did you get those? I'll tell,' she said primly.

'My father gave them to me,' he lied triumphantly.

It was during Picture Study that the disaster happened. He had been fiddling in his pocket all through the lesson during which they were supposed to notice the light and shade in the sepia tinted copy of Rembrandt's *Laughing Cavalier*. Suddenly a whoosh, a puff of smoke, a strong smell of sulphur, quickly followed by a spurt of flame, sprang from Gerald's pocket. Screaming, he began to dance wildly around the room until Suthy, with great presence of mind, pushed him over and whipping her scarf from her neck pressed it and herself on top of him until the fire was properly strangled.

A hysterical Gerald was taken by Annie into the night nursery and laid on Betty's bed, shortless, and his father sent for. Without a word, a pale, subdued Gerald, now in a new pair of shorts and mostly unhurt, was marched off to the car. His father looked more like the devil than ever with his black hair and frowning black brows.

'Was your father very angry?' she asked him in hushed tones next day but Gerald chose not to hear her.

Michael was a little boy from down the street, the same age as Baby. He had blue eyes and golden curls and was very pretty indeed. His fussy mother got very cross when they started to call him Micky and rang Mother to complain. She complained about a lot of things and after a while he stopped coming to lessons.

Suthy always had a task for each of them during the long summer holidays. One year Betty was asked to find a white bluebell. Father laughed about that. 'A white bluebell? A contradiction in terms, surely. Perhaps she means a white whitebell or maybe you could find a blue whitebell?'

Mother, who knew all about wild as well as garden flowers, asked, 'Does she mean a white wild hyacinth or a white harebell?'

Suthy explained that wild hyacinths came in all shades from white to deepest purple but as they were spring flowers they would all be over. Harebells were the proper 'Bluebells of Scotland' and August was when they flowered. A white harebell was very rare indeed.

Harebells grew everywhere at Shanwell, clumps of them in the hedgerows, on the hillside, in the heather. They were all blue, some a little darker than others, almost purple, but none was white. She could not imagine a white harebell. That summer, although she added to her wild flower collection, all she really wanted was to find the white bluebell. Then one day near the end of the holidays they were up at Golland Bridge for a walk with Annie when she said, 'Isn't that what you're supposed to be looking for?' and there it was, a clump of white harebells growing by the stile into the bull's field.

Mother found a little cardboard box and they packed just one slender stem with its cluster of little white bells and green buds between layers of damp cotton wool and posted it to Suthy. For a prize Suthy gave her the

37

Observer's Book of Wild Flowers which matched the bird book. Another set to collect, like stamps and elephants.

It was father who first collected stamps. He had a huge collection, part of which had been left to him by his best friend who had been killed in the Great War. Sometimes after tea instead of games, he would show it to the children who, of course, wanted their own collections. As he had plenty of spares he taught them how to soak the envelopes in a saucer of warm water to get the stamps off without tearing them, handle them with tweezers and fix the stamp hinges so that they stuck in the albums mother kindly bought for them. Betty and Bunty now spent part of their pocket money on little packets of used stamps which they swapped not without some arguments. Father thought them a waste of money which was true. Mostly they were all duplicates of what they already had. Gradually, however, their albums expanded. 'Great Britain' could have done with twice as many pages, and, strangely enough, there seemed to be plenty from 'Magyar' and 'Helvetia', and, of course Malaya where Uncle Alec lived. Stamps with father was fun, like going round the world.

The elephant collection started the year mother and father went to London. Father had been asked to preach at Evensong in Westminster Abbey because he was the friend and successor at Dundee of Provost (now Dean) Don. Mother went too and when they came back they brought each of them a present. Hers was a small elephant carved from of coconut wood with tusks and little white eyes made out of bone. She put it proudly on top of the bookcase in the night nursery.

Shortly after that, the two older sisters were taken as a treat to the Cathedral Summer Fete held in the big garden of someone in the congregation. She and Bunty were given 6d each to spend. Usually she made a beeline for the bran tub, where you pushed your hand into a barrel of sawdust and fished around for a little present. That cost 3d which left 3d for tablet. It was quite by chance that she saw the elephant on the Fancy Goods Stall. It was really small, but it looked exactly like hers, except that its tusks were missing. She wanted it badly but it cost 4d.

She wove her way through the crowd desperate to find one of her parents to lend her a penny before the baby elephant was sold. Mother was talking to Mrs Proudie, father's name for the Bishop's wife, and she had on her 'don't interrupt' face. She hung around for a while hopping from foot to foot but it was hopeless. She saw Bunty hovering around the Raffles table. 'Please, please, just a penny. I'll pay you back, I promise.'

Borrowing from Bunty was fairly hopeless at the best of times and on this occasion impossible because Bunty had already spent her whole sixpence. She had been persuaded by the verger, much against her will because Bunty was careful with money, to buy a raffle ticket with her remaining 3d. She was waiting patiently for the draw.

There was always father. She found him talking to three old ladies in fox fur collars and when she tugged his arm all he said was, 'Bye and bye, Betsy Jane'. 'Bye and bye,' meant 'I'm busy.' She wove her way back to the Fancy Goods Stall. The elephant was still there and it still cost 4d.

'All by yourself, young lady?' The aged dean towered over her. He too was on his own. His towering daughter who was known in clerical circles as the dean-ess and who taught her dancing was anchored to the cake stall. 'I know what you want,' he said triumphantly, 'a cup of tea. Follow me!'

She felt rather proud as she stuck close to his black heels as he furrowed a path between the crowds with a charming 'Excuse me - so kind - this young lady requires refreshment'. The tea marquee was heaving with people. Cathedral Ladies' teas were renowned in the city. He found one spare seat at a table with five other smiling be-jewelled ladies where he sat down thankfully (she had to stand) and when the waitress, another cathedral lady in an apron and a large straw hat, arrived to take his order he told her, 'tea for two, if you please, and 'your best cakes' she hadn't the heart to tell them she detested tea.

So she left it un-drunk hoping no one would notice. No one did. The dean was enjoying the undiluted attention of five ladies. After she had eaten a chocolate biscuit - the cakes were finished though one was hastily scrounged from another table for the dean - she would have liked to leave but she thought it might be rude.

Eventually she noticed that the tent was rapidly emptying. The raffle was about to be drawn. She excused herself politely, thanked the dean, who called her back, fumbled in his pocket and withdrew a shilling. 'Go and spend it for me, my dear, he told her pressing it into her hand. She could have kissed him. Instead she scuttled out as fast as she could, only to get snagged up in the crowd that had assembled round the platform with the raffles. There were some good prizes, she noticed, a large fussily dressed Spanish doll, a china plate with a horse painted on it, a cut-glass flower vase… She could see Bunty still hovering. The nice verger was in charge. The stubs of the tickets had been put into a biscuit tin, shuffled and the lady who owned the garden and wore a lot of floaty clothes asked to draw the lucky numbers.

'Excuse me, excuse me!' She pushed through the watching and clapping crowd to the Fancy Goods stall. The stall holders were beginning to pack up.

'What was that, my dear?' one of them shouted over a burst of clapping. 'Oh look, dear. That's your sister isn't it?'

She turned. Bunty was on the little platform accepting a large jar of boiled sweets, the likes of which she had only glimpsed on a shelf in the paper shop. Her first feeling was of undiluted envy. How had Bunty been so lucky? It wasn't fair. Second thoughts were of truculent admiration. Only Bunty could be so lucky. Third thought was triumphant. She'll have to share it this time. She can't eat them all by herself. Bunty was not too good at sharing. Well, to be honest, none of them were.

When the clapping had died down, she asked the lady at the stall about the elephant. 'Oh you mean the little coconut wood ornament? It was sold a while go, I'm afraid.'

She felt the tears watering her eyes. One of the two ladies in charge of the stall said, 'I'm so sorry, dear. We didn't know you wanted it'. They caught each other's eye, turned their heads away from her but she knew they were smiling.

How dared they laugh. Now she was in a mood. Jealousy and disappointment soured her expression. Mother with a triumphant Bunty clutching the large jar of mixed boilings came to find her.

'Time to go home. Have you got everything? Didn't Bunty do well?' Mother didn't notice that she said nothing. There was no need to speak. Bunty was jabbering away non-stop about her ticket, about what she had got in the lucky dip, the huge ice cream cone someone had given her.

'What did you buy?' Father asked mother, who was driving them home.

'A bit of everything, mainly plants for the garden and a baby jacket for Mrs Love's latest offspring.'

'And what about you, Betsy Jane?'

There was so much disappointment in her that all she could do was shake her head and mutter something about it all being rubbish.

'Really?' Father sounded surprised. 'You won't want this, then?'

He fumbled in the pocket of his black jacket and drew out a small tissue-papered parcel and handed it to her in the back of the car. 'I found it among the White Elephants. I thought it looked very out of place,' he said with a laugh.

She unwrapped the tissue and there it was, the tiny tuskless coconut wood baby elephant. That was how the collection started. Later when she had those teeth out, Annie and Hannah and mother and father, bought her four, one for each tooth, all different sizes. That summer Suthy went to South Africa and brought back two enormous matching elephants, one for her and one for Bunty. Without fuss, without really saying anything, Bunty let Betty keep hers which was beyond generosity. Now she had a proper collection that marched in single file along the top of her bookcase and everyone knew what to get her on special occasions. Still do.

Chapter Three

Passions and Pictures
Nine people lived in the house not counting God and the guardian angels. These were the people who inhabited her home but there were also the people who inhabited her heart.

It started at 'the pictures'. Annie and Hannah and Mina were always talking about 'the pictures'. Seemingly they went there on their days off. Suthy told them the story of Al Jolson and Sonny Boy and sang the song in her rather good alto voice which, she said, had made her cry. Betty was intrigued. What were these 'pictures'? Surely they must be more interesting than the *Laughing Cavalier*. Mother and father refused to discuss it. 'You're too young,' they told her dismissively as if that were the end of the matter.

So they nagged Annie instead. Every day it was 'Why can't we go?' 'Because you can't.' 'But why can't we?' Worse still Pam across the road, her new friend, was allowed to go with her big brother to Saturday matinees whatever they were. It was so unfair.

'All right,' aid Annie in her fed-up voice. 'I'll take you to 'the pictures'. Anything for a quiet life.'

Next afternoon instead of their usual walk round the Park or along the Perth Road or up to the Law Hill (very occasionally because it was a long way) they caught the

43

tram into town. After a short walk through the busy streets they came to a forbidding if imposing stone building 'This is it,' Annie told them and in they went. Room after room full of great dark paintings in heavy gold frames stared gloomily down at them. 'Is this really 'the pictures'?' She asked Annie. Her voice echoed in the cavernous gallery.

'See for yourself,' Annie said tartly. 'You asked. You got.'

Disappointment silenced her. That they were pictures, she could not deny, but there was something wrong. She could not imagine Annie and Hannah and Mina coming here every week and giggling over such mysterious names as Clark Gable and Gary Cooper in this boring place.

The experience silenced her for at least a week, or maybe only a day until she made the mistake of boasting to Gerald that she had been to 'the pictures'. For a moment he was interested, so she expanded. Gerald said scornfully. 'That's not 'the pictures', silly. That's the Art Gallery.'

'How do you know?' Gerald was not allowed to go to 'the pictures' either.

'I've been there loads of times. 'Pictures' is just a babyish name for the cinema,' he explained loftily. 'You really are silly.'

'I am not!' she denied hotly and another interminable argument broke out. But she knew he was right, that she had been fooled.

'I don't really see why I shouldn't be allowed to go to the cinema,' she said trying the word out on her mother.

'We'll see,' she was told which was a decidedly hopeful sign.

Sure enough, not long after that, her mother announced at Saturday lunch. 'There's a Shirley Temple film on at the *Playhouse Cinema*. I thought we might all go.'

'Father too?' She held her breath.

'Are you sure Shirley Temple is suitable for fathers?' he teased her mother.

Her excitement was unbearable. She chattered and fidgeted and bit her nails till it was time to leave. She was silent only when they entered the dark auditorium. In those days you always got two films for the price of one. The B film had started as they pushed their way into the gallery seats. The only resemblance to the *Laughing Cavalier* was the lack of colour. A story in black and white unfolded in front of her, a strange and frightening story. Suddenly the piano lid crashed down on the pianist's hands. Bunty, terrified, shot under the seat and hid her eyes but Betty was mesmerised by *The Hands of Orlac*.

Then the curtains closed and an organ rose up in front of the stage and the lights came on and father bought them all an ice cream tub from a girl in a brown and yellow uniform carrying a tray. Shirley Temple was utterly adorable with all those bouncy curls. From then on she craved curly hair. That was why Annie gave her the pompadour wig which she had ordered from a catalogue so she could have curly hair when she dressed up. Princesses had curly hair.

When the film was over and the lights came on Bunty stood up and said in a loud voice, 'Thank you, Shirley.' Fortunately no one, except mother and father, heard her.

When Disney's *Snow White* came to Dundee, their excitement was intense. The shops were full of the characters, little metal dwarfs, small cuddly dwarfs, large not so cuddly dwarfs with clothes you could take off and which cost a mountainous 7/6, sheet music with the songs arranged for beginners to play on the piano, film slides, colouring-in books, picture books, story books. *Snow White* mania infected the sisters who, all three of them, had their own closely guarded collections.

The great day came, queues stretched all the way round the cinema but fortunately mother had booked their seats. All week Betty had been building up to a cold. 'It's nothing', she insisted though her eyes and nose were streaming and her head bunged up and fuzzy, but, by Saturday, she had a temperature. Mother put her foot down. Though she argued and ranted and wept, she had to stay in bed. Annie read to her, Hannah made her favourite banana sandwiches, Father even came to sit with her for a while, but she was inconsolable.

Her sisters were full of it when they came home. She listened to their chatter with her head turned to the wall. 'Grumpy was best,' Bunty said. 'I liked Dopey,' Baby interrupted, 'no I didn't, I liked Sneezy best'.

'What was the witch like?' she asked moodily

'Really scary,' Bunty assured her. That was all she needed for the tears to start again. Scary witches featured in all her favourite fairy tales from *Hansel and Gretel* to *Baba Yaga*. It was enough to make you scream.

'We bought you a present,' Baby told her by way of consolation, dumping a parcel on her bed.

She unwrapped the gramophone record with the songs from the sound track on its two sides. It was almost worth missing the film for this treasure. Within days she knew them all by heart, every inflection and every note. She particularly liked singing the *Wishing Well* song in her bath because of the echo.

The next film she was taken to had been recommended by Suthy as educational. It was all about Disraeli who was acted by someone called George Arliss. He was not a young man, he was not a tall man, nor could you call him handsome, but she fell totally and absolutely head over heels in love with him. He stormed into her heart and stayed there. Princes and princesses vanished forever. Instead she became Disraeli's faithful servant who looked after him, became his confidante when he returned from Parliament tired and hungry, his nurturer, his favourite person in all the world. Disraeli had George Arliss's face.

Not long after that, George Arliss became *Cardinal Richelieu*, then *The Iron Duke* and *Dr Syn* and thus cemented into her imagination. He dominated her dreams, her chatter and her games. Mother and father teased her about him. Instead of sulking she basked in it. Mother got a book from *Boots* library about him. It was too difficult to read herself, but for some reason it contained his address, 14 Laughlin Place, Hollywood. She had no need to write it down for it had burned itself into her head. It was Hannah who suggested she write to him.

'Write to him?' she was intrigued.

'Write him a wee letter telling him you like his films.' A wonderful idea. So Hannah helped her. She sat at the kitchen table and in her very best writing she put 'aged nine' at the top by the address and the date. She would be nine in August by the time the letter arrived. He might not pay any attention to someone who was only eight years old.

She did not really expect a reply, but one day, months later, a typewritten envelope arrived addressed to her. Father who was sorting out the letters before breakfast handed it to her. All it contained was a black and white photograph of an elderly man with a monocle and scrawled across it the words, 'Best Wishes, George Arliss.'

Mother and father were not pleased that she had written without asking them about it, but they allowed her to keep the photograph. Mother even bought her a frame from *Boots* and she kept it on her bedside cabinet. Truth to tell, though, she preferred to think of him as *Disraeli* or *Cardinal Richelieu*.

Besides by now there was someone else in her heart. Mother decided she was grown-up enough to go to a lecture in the Caird Hall given by someone called Grey Owl. Pam was going too. She felt very grown-up going out with mother by herself, just the two of them. They sat in the middle of the auditorium which was very full. She could see Pam sitting with her brother and her mother several rows in front. There was a hush and suddenly on to the empty platform there strode a magnificent figure. Tall, wearing a full headdress of feathers that fell all the way down his back and a belted buckskin jacket with long fringes, a handsome deeply tanned man with piercing blue eyes strode forward, lifted his right arm and in a deep resonant voice called out 'How'.

The delighted audience howled back at him. She was struck dumb with adoration. He took off his headdress in compete silence while everyone stamped and clapped, then he turned to face the gathering, folded his arms and waited. 'Can you hear me, brothers?' he called out to the back of the auditorium. The shrieking and clapping burst out again and again he waited for silence. Then he began to speak. To be honest she was not much interested in what he had to say about beavers. It was him, every inch of his beautiful Indian majesty that stormed into her head.

Next day Pam boasted that she had waited at the stage door and got his autograph on her programme. 'He called me 'little sister'' she boasted showing her the indecipherable scrawl. Betty reproached her mother bitterly. 'Why didn't we get his autograph?' She was so disappointed that next time mother went down town she bought her a magical book that he had written called *The Tree*. It was full of drawings by him and it had a beautiful photograph of him that told her his real name was Wa-Sha-Quon-Asin which was Indian for Grey Owl. She whispered the strange name over and over again

Geroge Arliss aka Disraeli slipped quietly out of her head, his place to be taken by Grey Owl. She lived in his cabin, cooked for him, cared for his beavers, nursed him when he got a cold, and told herself interminable stories in which they rescued each other from floods and fires and enemy Indians. He always ended the adventure by telling her, 'What would I do without you, little sister?'

One morning at breakfast a year or so later while father was reading the *Times,* propped up against the marmalade pot, he exclaimed, 'Good Lord! Grey Owl's dead.'

She burst into tears and ran out of the room. Father came upstairs to console her, but, strangely enough, his death had no effect on the stories in her head. In a weird sort of way he became more hers in death than he had been in life where he belonged to everybody who saw and heard him. Now, as father said, he belonged to God and as she too was a child of God that somehow made them very close. The stories in her head carried on as usual.

Chapter Four

Auntie Meg

Not all deaths were like Grey Owl's. His had somehow had an enhancing effect on her feelings. Other deaths, however, could only diminish her outer life and her inner heart. Auntie Meg's was the first. Her absence made little change to daily routine. Suthy still taught in term time. They still went to Shanwell for holidays. At the same time everything was subtly different; lightless, as if the sun had gone behind a cloud.

Shanwell had two big bedrooms with a dressing room between them on the top landing at the front of the house facing south and perpetually bathed in sunshine. Mother and father shared one of the rooms and the dressing room. The other big room was reserved for father as a quiet place to say his 'words', or for any other visitor who might want to stay.

Auntie Meg had one of the two rooms off the lower landing. Both these rooms were largish but dark as they had only one small, deeply recessed window apiece which faced east and west. On the far side of her room, another door led down three little steps into the nursery wing where the children stayed with Annie. This had its own steep back staircase which led down to the one and only bathroom shared by everyone. The bath stood on its own clawed legs and most of the enamel had worn off but there was room in it for all three sisters at the same time. No one liked sitting at the plug end because when it was pulled up out you might be sucked down the black gurgling hole.

The east-facing room across the landing from Auntie Meg, known as the Blue Room, also had another door that opened into the servants wing, a warren of little rooms with their own staircase where Annie-the-Cook as opposed to Annie-the-Nanny and the various house- and table-maids lived. It was a no-go area for the children.

The main staircase curved downwards to a large rectangular tiled hall where the telephone was kept. Two shallow cupboards opposite each other held string and candles and drawing pins and screw drivers and always smelt sugary which made her think there were sweets there too. In fact, it was dry rot, but not recognised as such for at least another decade.

The hall opened into the porch where the coats, gumboots, walking sticks, dog leads and waterproofs hung higgledy piggledy around a large spotted looking-glass. Three reception rooms led off the hall. Once you had managed to turn the slippery handle and push through the heavy draught-proof curtain, the drawing room was a magical place, large, sunny, full of cabinets, beaded footstools, occasional tables, hard-backed chairs with barley sugar legs and dominated by a grand piano draped in a shawl and covered with silver-framed family photographs. Ornaments abounded. Her favourite was the set of intricately carved ivory Indian gods and buffalos and water-carriers, including, of all things, a snake-charmer. Trunk-loads of Indian art had been brought home from Poonah by Auntie Meg's sister, the children's grandmother, who had died when Betty was only three and it was all on display.

Even on the dullest day the crowded room appeared to be filled with sunshine and the scent of roses from the many bowls and vases which Auntie Meg picked from the garden under the reproachful eye of Mackenzie the gardener.

Beside Auntie Meg's chair was a wireless, a box with a trumpet attached to it. When she was very small she thought the wireless people lived in the box. She had grown to love the wireless, especially *Children's Hour* which had wonderful stories with characters called Larry the Lamb with his shaky voice and the gruff Mayor. Her favourite was Mole in the *Wind in the Willows*. The good of the wireless was you could listen to *Toy Town* and *Where the Rainbow Ends* in Dundee as well as Shanwell. She puzzled a great deal about how this could be possible.

The dining room was also the morning room where Auntie Meg wrote her letters. Betty loved to play with the little weighing machine which Auntie Meg told her was used in the 'olden days' to weigh letters for posting. The 'olden days' featured largely in Auntie Meg's stories of cousins and India and the war and how Granny was the first person to have a grown-up's tricycle in the county of Kinross. A grown-up's tricycle was almost inconceivable.

The billiard room, which was also the library, was behind the dining room. Here she escaped from time to

52

time to crouch under the great green baize table and look at back copies of the *Strand Magazine* with their creepy drawings of ghosts and murderers in dark places. A strange ornament stood on the mantelpiece which Auntie Meg said was an urn containing the ashes of a mother and baby who had died thousands of years ago. It had been dug up when workmen were constructing the East Avenue in the 'olden days'.

Two passages led from the hall, one to the tennis room, where croquet mallets and rackets, wickets and cricket bats were kept, while the other passage led past the flower room and the bathroom to the kitchen. It also led to the only lavatory in the house, a dark squalid cell with a wooden throne and a plug with a long handle and a faulty lock. It was the abode of all things nasty from beetles and spiders to snakes (probably) but, unfortunately, inescapable.

The kitchen was large, and, in spite of facing north, always seemed warm and sunny. It was dominated by a huge black range and a large red-faced woman, who wore white aprons and a white cap over her thin grey hair, called Annie-the-Cook. The kitchen was always the first place you visited when you arrived for the holidays and Annie-the-Cook the first person you hugged. Auntie Meg had to wait.

The children and Annie stayed with Auntie Meg all through the long lazy summers while mother and father either remained in Dundee or travelled north to visit father's family in Orkney. On these occasions when their parents were away, she was allowed to sleep in the dressing room at the front of the house because she was the eldest.

Summer mornings began at 7.30 am with Mackenzie raking the gravel underneath her window. Sometimes she would waken earlier and listen to the crows and the wood pigeons. There was one who called out 'Mont-mor-ency' over and over again and another who answered 'Not here, not here, not here'. Then she would quickly pull on her cotton dress with matching knickers and sandals, meet Auntie Meg in the porch, call the dogs who slept in baskets in the tennis room, and go outside to do the rounds.

Shanwell grounds were overgrown with high yew hedges, little paths that wound between shrubs and bushes, tall copper beeches, oaks and sycamores. Sweet briar hedges and crumbling walls made Shanwell the perfect place for hide and seek. Hidden among these delights, along a narrow winding path through the bushes, a wooden shed housed the petrol motor that provided electric lighting for the house. It was switched off every morning at 8 and switched on every night just before dark. It was a complicated noisy machine but Auntie Meg seemed to understand its eccentricities and most of the time the lights worked. She breathed in the heady oily petrol smell.

After that they went down to the tool-shed where Mackenzie was waiting to discuss the day's tasks. Sometimes Mackenzie would have Billie, his son, with him. He was pretending to teach him how to be a gardener, but Billie was much happier making mud pies on the bench. The smell of the tool-shed, damp earth and bone meal, was another delight.

Then they walked past the spout, where she stopped to drink a mug of the sparkling water that gushed out of a pipe the led underground from the Hurler hillside, always cold, always available. She and Bunty took it in turns to fill the water jug which stood on the dining room table for lunch. An aged pewter cup sat in a little stone alcove above the spout. Carefully she rinsed it and put it back where she had found it.

Then they walked round the back of the house to the courtyard to see Kirkwood.

Along with Suthy and Annie, Mr Kirkwood closely followed by Mrs Kirkwood were her favourite people after the family. He looked after the fences and ditches, hedges and water-gates, on Shanwell property. Sometimes they were allowed to go with him to choose the staples or hold the stob. Not often, though, because as Auntie Meg explained he had his work to do and the children held him up. Certainly they did. Kirkwood liked nothing better than to help her look for birds' nests or teach the three of them to skip stones. He was very good at it himself and his stones would skim down the Queich, up to fourteen times. She once managed five.

On Saturday afternoon, though, Kirkie was their's. He made little besoms for them to sweep the leaves, and whistles; allowed them, if they pestered him long enough, to take an end of the two-handled saw to cut up logs for the Big House. If it was wet and stormy he took them into his cottage and taught them how to play dominoes on the oilskin-covered table in front of the little black range where a kettle hummed contentedly all day long.

At the far end of the large woodshed, Kirkie kept his ferrets. She never grew to like ferrets with their endlessly long sinuous bodies, and sharp little teeth. They reminded her of snakes. Nor did she allow herself to think of how rabbit stew or roast rabbit regularly appeared at lunch time for she knew it was thanks to the ferrets, or worse, the traps. Kirkie kept his traps along with the ferrets at the far end of the woodshed. The smell of sawdust was another pleasure but if you went to the back of the shed you could smell the ferrets. They smelled of dentist's gas.

Mr and Mrs Kirkwood's two-roomed coachman's cottage stood at the entrance to a square cobbled courtyard. The court was Mrs Kirkwood's domain. Here her hens, her 'bonny bairns', scratched and fought and cackled endlessly. Mrs Kirkie was tiny with white curly hair and pale blue eyes. She always wore black pinnies sprinkled with little purple flowers, and ankle length black boots. Auntie Meg said she was a 'very superior' person.

After Auntie Meg had discussed with Kirkwood the tasks for the day, she found Mrs Kirkie in the bothy next to the woodshed stirring a great witches' cauldron of hen food. This consisted of oatmeal, tatties and the good scraps from the Big House kitchen and smelled much better than she knew it would taste. Mrs Kirkie supplied the Big House with eggs and boiling fowls. On rare occasions when she was 'no' busy' the children persuaded her to play with them. The game was always the same. She had to be a witch. She sat on a milking stool in the middle of the court with her eyes shut while they tried to flit from barn to byre, hen-house to wood-shed without her hearing them. She always did. The children reckoned she cheated.

Auntie Meg had a poke around the outhouses after she had spoken to the Kirkwoods. She even inspected the midden, a dump rarely used these days, but which also contained a shed with an outdoor lavatory, which Mrs Kirkie kept scrupulously clean. She was surprised to find bits of cut-up newspaper attached to a piece of string instead of proper Izal lavatory paper with its little messages on every sheet which she always read in the hopes of finding something interesting and never did

The smell of petrol delighted her all over again in the old stable which was now a garage. Sometimes Auntie Meg got the Austin out and together they would drive it round to the front of the house to await the morning shopping trip.

After a breakfast of porridge and eggs with Annie in the day nursery, and 'jobbies' done whether you needed to go or not, she and Bunty joined Auntie Meg in the morning room where she was finishing her letters. It was time to drive the three miles down to the village to get the messages.

Together with the dogs they scrambled into the car taking it in strict turns as to who was to sit in front. If there was any argument, the dogs took that coveted place and they both sulked behind, but not for long. Auntie Meg had a blistering tongue.

First stop in Kinross was Sands, the grocer. Sometimes Auntie Meg sat in the car outside the shop and hooted. Mr Sands himself came out in his long white apron and took her order. Once a month they went inside so that Auntie Meg could pay the bill. On these occasions Mr Sands produced a large sweetie jar and the children were offered one each. She loved that shop with its wonderful smell of coffee, bacon, cheese and biscuits.

Next door was the proper sweetie shop. Here Auntie Meg bought halfpenny bars of milk chocolate, one for each dog. The children were trusted not to nibble a corner but the temptation was great. There was never any question of buying chocolate for themselves even if they had 6d to spend.

Leaving the dogs in the car to savour their chocolate, they walked down the hill to Stillies, the paper shop. There were sweets here too and the shop smelt headily of sugar and newspaper. They spent their money on painting or puzzle books or a delightful storybook magazine called *Fairyland Tales*.

Sometimes on a Saturday morning they would stop by the church to help Auntie Meg arrange the altar flowers. It was the smallest church they had ever seen but special because there was a stained glass window by the family pew in memory of Auntie Meg's brother who had died when he was twelve. He would have been their Uncle Andrew if he had lived. All the men in Auntie Meg's family were called either George or Andrew. Some of them had grown to be very old. They stared down at her, benevolently unsmiling, from the drawing room and dining room walls.

Back by Milnathort, perhaps, for petrol and occasionally an ice-cream cone or a slider from the Italian ice cream shop with the impossibly spelled name which sounded like Jack-o-pie-zee. Then home in time for a rest on their beds with their new books before nursery lunch.

Every afternoon Annie took them for a walk. Sometimes they went up the High Planting through the noisy rookery and down the steep brae between the trees

58

to the bathing pool. This was a deepish, darkish, quiet stretch of water fed by a series of rocky rapids where on hot days they would sit and let the water try to carry their legs or stray fingers away. Sometimes they would paddle on the slippery stones or swing on the water-gate or sail paper boats, fish with worms on string lines or butterfly nets, and, if it was warm enough, bathe in the pool. It was just about deep enough for her to swim.

Other days they visited the two adjacent farms owned by Auntie Meg but let to Sam and Jimmy Forrester. Occasionally they would visit old Mrs Forrester who lived with the unmarried Sam, sometimes they saw young Mrs Forrester, whose name was Elsie and who was married to Jimmy. One day when they visited young Mrs Forrester, she was in bed, and, beside her, lay a newborn baby. The room smelt deliciously of baby and talcum powder and Mrs Forrester looked young and different with her hair all loose and laid out on her pillow. The baby was called Elma.

Annie did not go in to see old Mrs Forrester though. Annie liked Sam but old Mrs Forrester didn't like Annie. It was difficult to see why Annie would like Sam because he never spoke. He would nod his head if he passed them in his tractor, or give an answering wave if he was hoeing turnips, but he never said a word. Mrs Forrester had bad legs and sat all day in a chair by a coal range. She employed a girl called Mary to do the cooking and dairy work. Annie didn't like Mary because Mrs Forrester wanted Sam to marry her. The children did not much care to visit Mrs Forrester because they had to sit on a horse-hair sofa which scratched their legs, but she was very kind. She always gave them half-a-crown at the end of the holidays, and, if they visited after Christmas, a glass of sweet syrupy wine and a thick slice of black bun left over from New Year.

Sometimes they would walk up to Golland. This was a long trek through the hills to join the Queich higher up nearer its source. There was a little wooden bridge where they played Pooh Sticks for ages. That was where Annie had found the white bluebells.

Another walk was up the Hurlers and behind the New Plantation of dense pine trees at the edge of Auntie Meg's land. On the other side of the fence was a dilapidated cottage surrounded by trees. Old Bain lived here. They were scared of old Bain because he had a long reddish beard and he ate crows. Betty told Bunty and Baby that this was because he was a wizard. Annie may not have heard her, but if she did, she did not deny it.

The crow part was certainly true. Close to the back of his cottage there was a crow trap. This was a wire netting enclosure tall enough for a man to stand. In. the middle of the top of the enclosure was a funnel of netting and at the bottom a dead rabbit. The crow flew down the funnel to eat the rabbit but couldn't get up again. There was one flapping about as they watched.

'Why doesn't he eat the rabbit?' she asked Bunty who was equally horrified that anyone should go to such lengths to eat a crow.

'It's cruel,' Bunty declared. Together they hatched a plan. After tea, they would go back by themselves and set it free.

'What if old Bain sees us?' Bunty asked.

The cottage always looked deserted. She was not entirely sure she believed in old Bain, but the trapped

60

crow was real enough. 'Perhaps he'll be out,' she said encouragingly.

'Perhaps he's dead,' Bunty said and they both collapsed in giggles.

Auntie Meg had Cousin Mary and Cousin Martha from Elie to tea. She was not too much bothered when the children slipped away to play. Of course Baby wanted to come too. 'You're not to tell,' they both warned her. When they reached the edge of the trees, Baby found a rabbit warren and a lot of sand, sat down and refused to budge. 'Wait here for us,' they told her, and ran on.

There were now two crows in the trap. This was scary stuff. But there was no sign of old Bain, no smoke from the chimney. They squeezed through the wire fence and ran over to the trap. The crows flapped viciously and cawed loudly as the children fumbled with the latch and opened the netting door wide. Then they ran back to the safety of the fence and the shelter of the trees. From there they waited just long enough to see that the trap was empty.

Baby trailed and grizzled behind them all the way home, but that was fine. They were too full of triumph, virtue and power to complain. They arrived back just in time to wave goodbye to Cousin Mary and Cousin Martha who were trundling their old car down the east avenue. There was plenty of time for a game of *Spillikins* with Auntie Meg while Bunty and Baby had their baths.

They had, of course, been seen. Auntie Meg summoned them down from milk and biscuits in the nursery. She had just had the incandescent gamekeeper on the Calder estate on the telephone.

'Would Miss Coventry please explain to these children that the crows were a danger to his game chicks,' and a lot more beside which included vague threats that included a gun.

Auntie Meg was indeed angry, but not, it seemed, with them. She had had a running feud with the Calder estate for many years over boundaries. She explained that old Bain was in hospital. He had been a kindly old man who had shown her where to find mushrooms when she was young. Nor did she think there was much wrong with eating a crow if you were poor and hungry.

She came upstairs to read them a story as she did every evening when mother and father were away.. That was almost the best time of the day. She read books she had enjoyed as a child. One story in particular always made Betty cry. It was called *The Gentle Heritage* about a family of children who were scared of the old man next door because he wore a black patch over his eye. They thought he was a bogeyman but in reality he was brave and kind and good. A bit like old Bain.

One day, Auntie Meg had arranged to take them to St Andrews to meet cousins of their own age Unfortunately because she was unwell she had arranged for a taxi to drive them there with Annie and bring them back again. That was her first heart attack

Next day Mother came through from Dundee to take them home. They were back at Shanwell next spring and summer as usual, but they never saw Auntie Meg again. When Christmas came, she realised with sorrow that an absence could be almost as palpable as a presence.

Chapter Five

Dancing, Dresses and Saturdays

She never really got the hang of dancing. It was not that she did not love to dance. She would spend hours twirling and pirouetting around the nursery, lost in fantasy, to the music of the records she was given along with her beloved gramophone on her eighth birthday. *The Fairy Gavotte* was her favourite. She would glide gracefully around the room and down the passage, reach up on the tip of her toes and swoop her arms round and down in fairy-like flying gestures, breaking off only to wind the machine up before it slowed down in a hideous diminuendo. *The Dance of the Hours* on the other side of the record also provided some striking movements which in no way resembled the formal positions of dancing class, how to do the *pas de bas* or who to set to first in *Petronella*.

Every Tuesday, instead of lessons, they changed into dancing frocks, packed their bronze dancing pumps with little rosettes on the instep into special small cases and set off to the home of whoever was hosting the class that week.

The dancing mistress was Miss Macrae, the dean's daughter, known in the diocese as the dean-ess, or, in the nursery (if out of mother's hearing), as the giantess. She was vast, tall and broad as a tree in full leaf but she had twinkling feet. Betty knew this because all she could see of Miss Macrae was a pair of stout black-stockinged legs that seemed to reach up to the ceiling attached to huge, but incredibly deft, pink, ballet-slippered feet.

63

Nannies and mothers stood round the room eyeing their charges encouragingly and everyone else critically as they marched round the room or skipped in rhythm to the thump of the piano. She never really quite knew what she was doing.

When the classes were held in Broughty Ferry that meant tea afterwards at Forbes Court where the Bishop lived, and where Mrs Proudie presided over the teapot and particularly good meringues. Mrs Proudie had a purple face and always wore a silk toque. No one had ever seen her without it and the rumour was that she was bald. She ran the diocese in true Proudie style. Sometimes the bishop was there too but he never spoke. He was never given the opportunity. No one spoke much except, of course, Mrs Proudie.

One year Betty went to tap-dancing classes with Pam. She had a pair of red shoes tied with a red ribbon with hard heels and shiny steel caps attached to her toes. She loved tap-dancing but it was not much use at home because of all the carpets. The only place she could practise was in the bathroom which was too small, so she was sent to Eurhythmic classes instead. That was a disaster. The other girls were much older than she was and she never got the hang of it. The teacher put on a show in the Caird Hall and asked her, as the youngest in the class, to demonstrate one of the steps. She skipped hopefully and wrongly round the stage until one of the older girls came to her rescue. That, thankfully, was the end of Eurhythmics.

Dancing classes inevitably led to parties and parties meant party dresses.

On some Saturday mornings the nursery was given over to Miss Mathieson, the dress-maker, who sat in front of a Singer sewing machine at the white nursery table among swathes of material, pin cushions and paper patterns. She was a cross, busty woman with a round pink face and rigidly curled iron-grey hair. She was not to be trusted with pins.

Mother preferred to dress them alike. Most of the time she and Bunty were content to wear Fair Isle jumpers and kilts in winter, cotton dresses over matching knickers in summer which Miss Mathieson cut out, stitched and didn't prick you if you stood absolutely still, which meant, more or less, not breathing. Only once did they rebel.

A member of the congregation specialised in making lace collars and cuffs. Mother was entranced. She had an image of her three daughters looking adorable at dancing classes in velvet dresses with lace collars. The only snag preventing the dream from becoming reality was the cost of velvet. Not to be deterred, she found among the bales of cheaper materials a roll of what looked like rich blue velvet at a price she could afford.

Miss Mathieson sniffed and pointed out that the slippery man-made stuff would drag. The girls were more explicit. Betty could not bear to touch it. 'Ugh, it's horrid.' She squirmed. 'It sets my teeth on edge,' said Bunty. But the dresses having been made, had to be worn. They hung awkwardly, creased untidily, marked easily and caused an argument with Annie every time they were worn. But, as mother said, the pale coffee-coloured lace collars were beautiful.

Perhaps to make up for that disaster, mother went to town on their party dresses. This time they submitted with uncharacteristic patience as Miss Mathieson measured and pinned and sharply manoeuvred their limbs. The resulting puffed skirts and puffed sleeves of fragile pink voile, sprigged with tiny embroidered rosebuds over underskirts of taffeta, were worth the trial. They rustled and bloomed becomingly, or so Betty believed, at the usual round of Christmas parties.

The excitement of anticipation before a party never quite matched the reality. The pattern seldom varied. *Pass the Parcel, Musical Chairs, Musical Statues, Mulberry Bush* were good games at which she tried her utmost, but never won. There were good prizes too. Sometimes there was a conjuror, or sometimes flickering cartoon films. She loved Mickey Mouse but she could never see anything particularly funny about Charlie Chaplain. She noticed that only the grown-ups laughed.

If there were younger children present, they played *Musical Bumps* and *Oranges and Lemons* and the *Grand old Duke of York* which were fun. You could fool around a bit. Sometimes, though, she was asked to parties for older children where they played a nightmare game called *Forfeits*. A parent spun a plate and called out a name. If that person caught it before it stopped spinning they were clapped, but if not, they had to do something public and dreadful, like bow to the wittiest and, horrors, kiss the prettiest girl or handsomest boy in the room. The only time her name was called out she had to blow up a balloon till it burst. Fortunately someone's father put his lighted cigarette to it and put an end to her scarlet agony.

The most memorable party she ever went to was at the Guilds. They were cathedral people and great friends of mother and father. They had two older boys who paid them no attention at all and a girl called Valerie who was Bunty's friend. They also had a very fussy Nanny with a strange, strangulated, high-pitched voice. Valerie spoke exactly like her.

When they arrived the party had started. The carpet had been removed from the drawing-room for the usual games, and the spacious hall had been rearranged. At one end there was a long table like a shop counter stocked with new toys. You had to find tiddly-wink counters hidden throughout the downstairs rooms, and, with them, you could buy these toys. There were dolls, cars, trains, puzzles, books and bricks, also a little yacht, she deeply coveted, worth one red or two blue counters. But the counters were not easy to find. Other children who had arrived earlier were already queuing up to spend what they had found. She searched behind chairs, under the hall table, in the cloakroom. Nothing. The game was nearly over when Mr Guild came up to her and whispered, 'I suggest you try under the hat-stand.' Sure enough. One red counter. She clutched it and ran to the toy store but the yacht had gone and so had most of the other toys. A few jig-saws remained. 'You can have two for a red counter,' Mrs Guild told her. Just in time, she remembered to say 'thank-you'.

After that, the party got a bit out of hand. Perhaps it was because Valerie's brothers who were big boys got rough. '*A-Dree a-Dree I Dropped It*' was rough anyhow. Someone ran round a circle of children tapping, or, in Nigel's case, bashing them all on the head with his shoe.

He dropped it behind Bunty's back which meant she had to run round the circle after him. Somehow in the ensuing chase he caught hold of her beautiful rose-bud dress and ripped the skirt half off. She minded, so Nanny Guild took her up to the nursery and consoled her with biscuits until it was time to go home.

The rosebud dress was easily mended but somehow never completely trusted again. Not like the hated indestructible gaiters. Going out in winter was a palaver. First you had to take off your indoor shoes and your pinafore. Then it took hours, or so it seemed, to pull on the thigh-high fawn leg covers and do up the innumerable side buttons. Outdoor shoes had to be laced and sometimes the knot went wrong. Tweed coats, gloves and tammies, or felt cloches on winter Sundays, panamas in summer, completed the outfit.

Dressing in the morning was tricky too. They were not allowed to get up before 7 30 but sometimes Betty would waken long before that, impatient to get on with the day. Whoever was dressed first had their hair done first by Annie, so she would sneak her combinations off her bedside chair and surreptitiously try to put them on under the bedclothes without Bunty noticing. She nearly always did and would shout out to Annie next door, 'Betty's dressing!'

It was all right for Bunty and Baby, they both had short hair with only slides to fix but hers was long and fine and tangly and had to be plaited each morning, fixed with a rubber band and tied with a ribbon which was a long, painful and time-consuming process. She hated to be last in the morning, dressing, hair, breakfast. It was different at night. She was the eldest so she should have her bath last, her story and her light off last, that was only fair. Fairness was all.

Stories varied but the ones she liked best came from the coloured fairy books. One story in particular from the *Orange Fairy Book* called *Pinkel and the Witch* she could almost read herself. She preferred stories with wicked characters and Pinkel's witch was satisfyingly evil. Unfortunately witch stories gave her nightmares. Snakes, witches, ghosts and the creepy illustrations from the *Strand Magazine* all gave her nightmares. When, cackling, hissing, moaning, the monster closed in on her heels, she would rush through to Annie, gabbling, 'Can I come into your bed?' and a sleepy Annie would move sufficiently to let her crawl into the warmth and safety of her narrow bed, unless, of course, Bunty or Baby had got there first. They all had nightmares.

They found their own comforters. With Betty it was her blanket which she started to suck the moment the light went out, savouring the feel of the wool in her mouth and the faint taste of camphor and soap. Annie would tut a bit about the little suck marks all over the exposed end of her blanket and warn her that her tummy would be filled with little woolly balls. She also bit her nails which was considered to be much more serious. Mother tried bitter aloes, but she got quite to like the taste. Bunty sucked her thumb and Baby her first finger. That was really serious. She was pulling her teeth forward. On Doctor Kerr's advice Mother tried everything from bitter aloes to putting Baby's arm in a splint. Her pitiful sobs haunted her sisters long into the night.

Dr Kerr was also a cathedral member. He was a blunt jolly person with a very loud laugh and a strong Scottish accent who dominated the nursery on the few occasions Mother had cause to call him in. He teased Annie, joked with the children, and occasionally dined with mother and father They always knew when he came to dinner because his booming laugh ascended to the nursery. Everyone liked 'the Pill', as they called him, except for Betty. She hated him.

Usually a dose of syrup of figs or milk of magnesia cured whatever small ailments the children might have, but, on this particular occasion, mother was extra vigilant because Bunty had had a sore tummy which had ended in having her appendix out. The Pill stumped up the stairs wheezing a little and exuding bonhomie. Betty's nightie was lifted and he began his probe. His only comment to Mother was, 'She's awfu' fat'.

When the family teased her she was furious. 'I'm not fat. I'm not! I'm not!'

Mother made it worse. 'Of course not, darling. It's just puppy fat. Nothing to worry about.'

For the first time in her life she was aware of her own body. Perhaps she was a bit fat. Being fat was not good, on a par with sin. She did have a bit of a tummy, certainly. She noticed it for the first time at the swimming baths.

On Saturday mornings when Miss Mathieson was not needed, mother took them to the baths. She wore a navy blue woollen suit which outlined her big tummy. They all had swimming lessons and then splashed about in the shallow end in a rubber ring and a rubber bathing cap, and shouted 'Look at me!' just to hear the echo of their own voices. After a while she was confident enough to dive off the low springy diving plank, careful not to belly-flop, and even jumped off the high diving board.

Every Saturday she eyed the ropes. These hung down from the ceiling at intervals over the deep end and you were supposed to swing from one to another then back again without letting go. She tried but somehow never got the knack. She fell with a splash every time she tried to transfer from the first rope handle to the next. To add to her frustration, other children managed it easily, swinging like monkeys across the pool.

It occurred to her that perhaps she had weak arms, or, more likely, it was because of her fat tummy. This did not lessen her determination. With the other children she queued up for the rope and once, just once, she managed to transfer to the second rope. Coming back, however, was disastrous. Her arm gave out and she fell, hitting the sharp edge of the pool with her ribs. It was agony. Dr Kerr came and stuck a wide plaster round her body, front to back. It was still sore when she laughed or coughed and she couldn't bend properly for weeks. But that was nothing to the pain of having the plaster removed. She never much cared for the baths after that.

On Saturday afternoons Betty had piano lessons. Miss Fraser lived near enough for her to walk there on her own. She had a neat little house opposite the park on the Blackness Road and a stifling hot sitting room, a lot of pot plants and an upright piano with a metronome on top. She learned scales and chords and some very tricky exercises from the Czerny book and memorised short pieces which never seemed to match up to their intriguing titles, like the *March of the Dwarfs* or *Elfin Bells.* Miss

71

Fraser wrote down in a notebook what she had to practise at home. She was a little afraid of Miss Fraser, who, though she was small and had lots of real curly hair, held a ruler which she threatened to use if Betty proved she had not practised. Only once had she cause to use it.

The day was hot. Betty dawdled along the road swinging her leather music bag and dodging the pavement lines. She noticed that the tar nearest to the gutter had melted into little black bubbles that demanded to be pricked. So she did, breathing in the delicious smell of melted tar on her fingers, which, to her consternation, wouldn't wipe off. She rang Miss Fraser's doorbell then hid her hands behind her back, but of course her teacher noticed. She was very angry and rapped her hard across her tarry palms with her ruler, then she took her through to her kitchen and rubbed her fingers with butter until most of the mess came off and gave her a glass of lemonade.

The worst thing Miss Fraser made her do was an exam. Grade One. She was not sure what an exam or a grade was. Mother drove her to the Town Hall. There were lots of children waiting, some of them Miss Fraser's pupils. Eventually she was summoned into a large room where two unsmiling men sat at a table and told her to go to the grand piano which stood proudly on a platform by itself. She managed the scales a bit shakily then came to her set piece. *Fairy Lullaby.* Her hands were shaking so hard that the notes came out clashingly wrong. One of the men said kindly, 'Perhaps you would like to start again.' So she did, and yet again, but it never came out right. The annoying thing was she could play the piece note perfect in the drawing-room when she was by herself. Afterwards

Miss Fraser said very little but fortunately there was no more talk of exams.

One Saturday not long after the baths incident Father thought she might like to learn the organ. The way he asked expected the answer yes, so, as he had business in the cathedral with Mr Cow, the organist, he would take her himself. 'Cow?' she asked. They looked at each other and he laughed. 'But he doesn't moo...much. You'll like him.'

She did. Mr Cow was old and kind, too kind to be a good teacher. She sat beside him behind the blue curtain in the organ chamber, facing three manuals which was bewildering and a battery of stops which she could hardly reach. Nor could she reach the foot pedals. On that first day he showed her how to cling on to one note while you played the second, the very opposite of what Miss Fraser had taught her. She tried out *Fairy Lullaby* while Mr Cox reached over her to pull out the right stops and it sounded wonderful.

When father came for her she made him listen while she played it again. This time Mr Cox sat beside her and pumped the foot pedals. 'Please, please, please, can I come again?' She asked the two men.

Mr Cow nodded and beamed. 'Of course. Of course. She has a real gift, Provost.'

Father was pleased. She had one more lesson and then Mr Cow got ill and retired so that was the end of the organ.

Chapter Six

Friends, Godparents and Dogs
Father and Mother had not been young when they married. Both had hosts of friends who came for visits either to Shanwell or to Dundee where they stayed in the spare room, some for longer than others. Favourite among mother's friends at Shanwell was Janet.

Janet had been brought up at Thomanean, a neighbouring estate to Shanwell, and she had known mother from childhood. She now lived in London but she always came to Kinross for the summer where she stayed in the *Green Hotel*. Janet was stick-thin, her hands were purple and twisted with arthritis and she always looked ill, but, as mother said, looks can be deceptive. Janet was hardy and she was fun. She spent a lot of time at Shanwell and invited some or all of them to lunch at the *Green* at least once a week.

Janet could never make decisions. She would shilly-shally for ages over the menu, then when the meals came she would inspect them all and say, 'Yours looks nicer than mine.' The waitress was summoned and told to take her dish away and bring her something else. This caused shocked hilarity among the children because it broke all the nursery laws, but no one minded, least of all the waitresses who knew Miss Reid's little ways, and because she tipped well.

Mother told them Janet could have married a dozen times, but could never make up her mind who to choose, so she was a spinster, but she didn't mind in the least and even laughed when she lost at *Old Maid.*. She was Baby's

74

godmother, and, because Baby asked, she gave her a dog for her birthday. Phillip and Charlotte having both died, mother and father welcomed the little Dandy Dinmont puppy into the household. Baby called him Tigger because he was so bouncy.

Mother and Baby adored Tigger but no one else did. He was snappy and cross and he bit you if he got a chance. Truthfully Betty did not like dogs. Suthy's wire-haired terrier chewed her toys; Auntie Meg's dogs had both been too old to play. The farm collies barked at her and Tigger bit. She preferred cats.

Janet had a brother called Robert who bred prize bulls on his farm and who once took the children for a drive in his new car at 100 miles per hour. She had an older sister called Maria who lived in a big house called Duncreivie and a younger sister who had a son called Maxwell whom secretly Betty much admired. They were all very well-off, having made their money in tea, or so mother said. That used to be a puzzle to her. How did you manage to make money in tea? She hated tea.

Another of mother's friends was called Helen. They had been at school together. She was pretty in a fluffy way and giggly and when she came to visit in Dundee she and mother would go down town a lot. She had a very fat black Scottie who slept on her bed and climbed onto her lap at meal times and begged for scraps, which he was always given. Helen talked to him in baby language which made the children want to giggle, but Helen was nice. She played *Snap* and *Beggar my Neighbour* with them and always lost; properly lost, without trying to lose. She was one of Bunty's godmothers. Father liked Helen too which could not be said of all mother's friends,

75

even after she had left and the wardrobe in the spare room was found to be full of empty gin bottles.

He did not particularly care for Auntie Sine. She was a large, clever, organising and extremely religious. When she agreed to be Betty's godmother she was 'high' Episcopalian but since then she had become a Roman Catholic and she was always trying to convert mother. Father too. 'It's just a matter of time before he sees the light,' she would say in a lordly fashion which annoyed mother but made father laugh.

There was no mistaking her kindness. She lived in the Black Isle with her mother and father who had served in the army with the children's grandfather. Two years running, after Auntie Meg's death, Betty and Bunty stayed with them for two weeks while Baby went north to Orkney with mother and father. Auntie Sine's mother had hundreds of dogs, or so it seemed, snappy little cairns, but they stayed in kennels at the side of the house so she rarely saw them. On her way to bed, Auntie Sine always looked in to see if they were asleep. Betty knew it was her by the glow of her cigarette which bobbed up and down in the dark room.

Before breakfast, Major Stuart took them down to the foot of his orchard and told them each to choose one apple off the tree. This was considered a great concession because the Major hoarded and counted his apples. They were expected to eat them on the spot, but, although they looked rosy and ripe, they were hard and sour and it was difficult not to make a face.

They were sent to the Episcopal church with someone called Jeanie Vee who was large and kind, and, as Auntie Sine said, had never 'grown up properly'. She took them out before the sermon and they climbed carefully down the steep steps on to the beach below the church on the cliff. Jeanie Vee said, 'I like it when you come because I don't like sermons'.

Nor do I, she thought, but she didn't quite like to say so. 'I like some sermons,' Bunty said diplomatically. Jeanie Vee thought for a while and then agreed. Then the children tucked their cotton dresses into the knickers and had a paddle. The gritty sand was horrid, though, full of bugs called sand-hoppers.

Father's friends were all quite old like Auntie Maimie. She had been father's mother's companion and when her employer died had elected herself to be father's housekeeper in his first Scottish parish in Aberdeen. She too was very large and wore lots of gold rings with purple and red jewels which had embedded themselves into the soft flesh of her fingers. She came from Hastings and did good work in the Mission to Fisher-girls

She looked cuddly and smelled nicely of eau-de-cologne but appearances were deceptive. Auntie Maimie was very critical over things like table manners and not speaking until spoken too. As mother said, she had very high standards. Strict she may have been but Father always managed to make her laugh. She adored father, and Bunty too, not so much because she was her godchild, but because she looked like Father.

She was very keen on music and asked questions like, 'What do you think of Dvorak's New World Symphony?' or 'have you listened to Beethoven's Ninth?' When Betty looked blank she told mother the children were musically illiterate.

Auntie Maimie always sent hankies for Christmas.

Most of father's friends were priests. Two were special. Peter Wilson was probably his best friend. He was rector of All Saints in St Andrews, a glittery, mysterious church always dim with incense. He had married father and mother and he had baptised Bunty. He joked and teased with the children in a kind way and made them giggle. He had two daughters both older than Betty, who were thought to be vastly clever, and a wife considered rather fast, because she was very pretty, Scandinavian and played bridge.

Another priest friend who visited every year was the Bishop of Bermuda. She never knew what his proper name was. He made a great fuss of the children and once insisted on taking all three of them by themselves to the cinema to see *Three Smart Girls*. He wore his full Episcopal dress, black frock coat, gaiters and a purple stock which caused a lot of stares when they entered the auditorium and not a few barely-suppressed giggles. He was very kind and bought them all ice cream tubs in the interval.

Uncle Sydney sometimes visited from Guildford where he lived with Aunt Elsie who seldom came with him, and a grown-up son. He was not a priest but he was what father called 'a keen churchman'. He and father climbed hills together which was not often because they were both so busy. He was large, wore loud tweeds, smoked cigars and drank whisky. Both mother and father enjoyed his visits which were all too short. Rules were relaxed when Uncle Sydney was around and he tipped both the children and the servants incredibly generously when he left.

Though he was Betty's godfather he sometimes forgot this and thought he was Baby's godfather, but Betty didn't really mind because he treated all the children the same.

Father had three brothers, one older called Uncle Pat who was a lawyer and two younger, Uncle Alan who was an architect in London and Uncle Alec, an engineer, who had spent his working life building the Burma railway. Every August they and their wives gathered together in the family home in Orkney which now belonged to Uncle Pat. They had had an older sister called Auntie Flo who had been Betty's other godmother but sadly she died of cancer when Betty was three.

The most important person in father's family had been his grandfather, John Mason Neale. He had been a priest who had written dozens of books and over seventy hymns in the English Hymnal. During a boring sermon she had once looked them all up and counted them. Sometimes the congregation sang them. She particularly looked forward to Palm Sunday when they processed round the cathedral after the choir singing *All Glory Laud and Honour* and holding their little palm crosses.

John Mason Neale also wrote books for children. Her favourite was *The Egyptian Wanderers* which was about Christian children crossing the desert and being chased by Roman persecutors. Father was very proud of his grandfather and so they all were too. He was the family hero.

After Auntie Meg died, apart from some oldish cousins, mother had only her younger brother left. Uncle Bob had been a major in the army in India before his posting to Canada where he met his wife, Aunt Nell, who was very smart and sophisticated and petite. They had one little daughter called Jill, whom the children had yet to meet.

Although he had inherited Shanwell, because he was mainly overseas, he was seldom able to visit. He was grateful to mother for keeping an eye on it and encouraged her to stay there whenever she wished. Uncle Bob was very shy, he giggled a lot and was exceedingly handsome. Mother adored him. He was Bunty's godfather.

Mother and father also had mutual friends they had made after they were married. One of these was called Dorothy Dundas. She lived in a big house in Stirling with a very good cook and when mother got seriously ill, not long after Baby was born, it was 'Dee Dundas' who came to the rescue. She took mother in and cosseted her in the greatest of luxury until she was well enough to come home. Father always went to her for a day or two after the big festivals of Easter and Christmas for a rest. She was Baby's other godmother.

These were the people whose love they took for granted, accepted without question, a part of the structure of their lives. There was also Annie. It was agreed among the children that Betty was mother's favourite, Bunty was father's favourite and Baby was Annie's. This caused no rancour between them. It was fair. If anything, Betty and Bunty were slightly jealous of Baby, who had been Annie's baby from the beginning.

Annie had started work as a maid at Shanwell when she was sixteen, a tall gawky girl with sloping shoulders and black curly-hair and brown eyes very like her father who was known as 'old Fowlis', a gardener, who came to live in the Lodge when Mackenzie left.

She had two sisters called Liz and Meg and a brother called Arthur. The ramifications of their families were on-going and fascinating. There was Annette who was red-haired and beautiful and little Arthur and the twins. Annie might have married Sam, if she had not been so busy with the children and Sam's mother had approved of her. As it was, she was deeply cherished by the children, the most important person in their lives on a par with their parents, and indispensable to mother especially after father became ill in the summer after Auntie Meg died.

Ah, father's illness…

Chapter Seven

The Wee Hoose

When father was diagnosed as needing three months complete rest, they all went to Shanwell for the whole summer. Without Auntie Meg, there were changes, some small, some enormous, only a few for the better.

The petrol machine no longer worked so they used lamps and candles instead of electric light. Lamps were hard work; the glass chimneys had to be cleaned regularly, the wicks trimmed, the oil renewed. Not to be trusted with lamps, the children had candles when necessary but the long light summer nights usually provided enough light until well past bedtime.

Annie-the-Cook had retired. Annie-the-Nanny's mother and sisters looked after the house when it was empty and agreed to come in and help out during the summer. Otherwise it was just Annie and Hannah and mother of course, but mother had her hands full with father.

The rooms were re-arranged. Father and mother moved into the other front room leaving the master bedroom and the dressing room for Uncle Bob, Aunt Nell and Jill should they wish to visit. Betty had the large nursery to herself. Bunty moved to Auntie Meg's room and Baby had the little night nursery. Annie moved into Annie-the-Cook's room up the back stairs. She no longer belonged exclusively to the children. She was far too busy.

The children shifted from their nursery playground to a clearing in the beech wood along the tennis-walk behind the house. There was a small wooden shed in the clearing, a perfect playhouse.

'Can we have it?' Betty implored the grown-ups. 'Please, please,' the others echoed. Mother came to look at it. No one seemed to know why it was there and no one used it. 'I don't see why not,' she agreed.

But it was too tall, too narrow and too dark, more of a storeroom really, a cupboard in search of a house. The house, she announced grandly, they would build themselves. They swept up the leaves with their besoms, picked out the weeds, collected bits of wood and stones, and started.

Mr Kirkwood passed while they were trying unsuccessfully to balance one stone on top of another. He pushed his cap back on his head, dropped his tool-bag and watched them for a few minutes.

'If it's a wee hoose ye're efter, that's no' the wye,' he said after a while, 'and,' he added, 'that's no' the richt place'.

They turned to stare at him. Betty opened her mouth to ask but there was no need.

'Ah'll get ye some stobs,' he said.

It took three days, working in his own time, after his tea, to finish the small log cabin. He built it under a thick beech branch which would help to keep out the rain. He roofed it in flat planks covered with 'trepalian' (tarpaulin, mother said), and cut out a little window. The plank door even had a handle. Mother found old bits of carpet and Mrs Kirkie found a spare milking stool in the bothy which no one used because the cow had long gone.

They pinned a couple of picture postcards of Orkney on the walls and filled a jam-jar with wild flowers which stood in one corner because there was no room for a table, barely room for the three of them to crowd in, but that was all right. They preferred to be outside. There was so much to do, most of which centred round the fireplace.

Annie showed them how to build a hearth in the middle of the clearing away from the trees in a circle of stones. They collected twigs and they were given a box of matches which they were warned not to waste and which they kept on one of the shelves in the shed, along with a few potatoes, some old cutlery, crockery and newspaper for kindling.

The fire was the best bit of the Wee Hoose. They lit it every day, taking it in turns to feed it with dry sticks, poking it till the sparks flew, burying potatoes in its hot depths (they were always raw inside) and occasionally cooking sausages on sticks watching the fat spurt and spit as it dripped from the meat. At the same time they acted out fantasies which sometimes involved Nelson (Bunty) and Napoleon (Baby) and herself as the Duke of Wellington, or, more often, American Indians surviving in the forests while wicked cowboys surrounded their camp.

The clearing was surrounded by old beech trees whose silver-smooth trunks where they entered the earth split into little rooms which they cleaned of dead leaves and lined with moss and created into fairy palaces.

Best of all was the graveyard. The clearing extended to the other side of the dirt path through the woods. One day they found a dead crow in the clearing. 'Let's bury it,' Betty said, 'properly'. They borrowed a trowel from the tool-shed and dug into the soft mulchy earth. There were too many roots to go deep, so the resulting grave humped up a bit. They surrounded it with a neat pattern of stones and made a cross with two pieces of the straightest sticks they could find, binding them together with a bit of string. Betty pinched a little wooden label from the tool-shed and wrote. *Crow RIP*. Bunty filled a jam-jar with buttercups from the Hurlers. Then they gathered round, folded their hands and repeated the Lord's Prayer. It all felt wonderful, beyond fun.

If you were looking, you could find dead creatures everywhere. A hedgehog on the side of the road, a tiny chicken among Mrs Kirkie's recently hatched pullets and a fledgling blackbird rescued from one of the farm cats. Each had its grave, its stone perimeter, its stick cross and its wild flowers in a jam-jar memorial. The graves were arranged in a horseshoe, twelve of them by the end of the summer, round a cleared space. It looked beautiful.

She got quite good at the prayers, too, in spite of the fact that she had never been to a funeral service, not even Auntie Meg's.

After all that work, they wanted to show the graveyard off, so Betty suggested 'a garden party and we'll dress up'. Written invitations went to mother and father to Annie and Hannah to Mr and Mrs Kirkwood and to Old Fowlis and Mrs Fowlis and Little Arthur who sometimes stayed with them.

They begged a bottle of squash and some more cups to add to the three handle-less rejects they kept in the shed. Hannah kindly made fairy cakes with hundreds-and-thousands sprinkled on the top which they set out on a card table borrowed from the drawing-room. Baby wore her boy shorts with proper flies and her toy pistol fixed to a leather belt. Bunty put on her flared shorts and slung her bow and arrow over her shoulder. Betty dressed up a princess in her longest nightie and her pompadour wig. Mother wore a straw hat and father put on a collar and tie. The sun shone between the beech trees and everyone came except for Old Fowlis. They stood around and admired the graves and she felt it had been a success in spite of the wasps.

She believed that Auntie Meg would have approved.

Chapter Eight

Birthdays

All her birthdays she could remember had been spent at Shanwell. Birthdays stood apart from the rest of the year, lit up in her mind like the *Playhouse* cinema on a winter's day.

Baby was born on Palm Sunday in 1931. Her birthdays often coincided with fast days and sometimes even fell on Good Friday, but, as she had been born on a Sunday, she was, according to the old rhyme, 'the child that is born on the Sabbath Day is bonny and blithe and good and gay'. Enviable, really. Bunty was six days later on the 4th April, a Thursday in 1929, so, although she had 'far to go' she suffered from the same bad timing, sometimes in the holidays, sometimes not, sometimes even on Easter Day which was a waste because Easter was already special. Mother's was July 15, better but not perfect. It nearly always rained. Father's was in October, Annie's in November but hers was in August, the perfect month because it was always in the holidays and always spent at Shanwell. Born on a Tuesday meant that she was 'full of grace' whatever that meant. If she had had a choice in the matter, she would have chosen a Monday, because 'Monday's child is fair of face'.

The shape of the day seldom varied. Breakfast with the grown-ups and then presents. One year it was a watch, a small round silver dial with proper numbers, a second hand and a black ribbon strap and it had her initials on the back. All she had to do was remember to wind it up every evening, and, because she was so conscious of its neat shape enhancing her wrist, she seldom forgot.

If it was fine, and it nearly always was, they played croquet on the lawn more amicably than usual. You certainly didn't fight or argue on your birthday and no one else did either. You were given-into over everything and that was a good feeling. Then you played with your presents until lunch, that special lunch for which Mrs Kirkie always provided, as a gift, her plumpest most succulent capon reared from a day-old chick. Cooked to perfection with roast potatoes, bread sauce, stuffing, bacon, sausages and the first new peas from the garden, she was allowed to carve it herself and have the wishbone.

Auntie Meg usually organised a party for her of local children in the garden with *Hide-and-Seek* and *Tracking*, her absolute favourite game where the leader laid out a trail of arrows made with sticks or chalk or pebbles or stuck little notes to hedges or trees and the trackers had to follow. Sometimes the leader laid a false trail and marked its end with a circle and a cross in it, so the trackers had to go back to the beginning. There were prizes and a cake with candles.

Once Auntie Meg, who was a keen fisherwoman, had taken her and Bunty perch-fishing in a boat on Loch Leven as a birthday treat. To her pride and delight, she had caught two perch but Bunty caught a salmon. There was no time to enjoy it because the boatman immediately unhooked it and threw it back into the loch. 'Why?' they asked indignantly. 'Perch fishing excludes salmon,' Auntie Meg answered cryptically. The perch were inedible.

Another year they were rowed across Loch Leven to the Castle Island to explore the ruins where poor Mary, Queen of Scots had been imprisoned. The midges were dreadful.

When Auntie Meg had gone, they usually had a family picnic taking the car high up into the Ochils or perhaps to Rumbling Bridge, which had the added fascination of being where some murderer was supposed to have cut up his wife and thrown the bits into the water. There was a scary song about it which Hannah taught her which went something like, 'Red stains on the carpet,/ Red stains on the knife,/ Oh bad Doctor Crippen,/ You've murdered your wife'.

On her ninth birthday, she only just made it to Shanwell. Mother and father had taken both Bunty and Florence to Orkney for a fortnight, Annie was on holiday and she had been invited to stay with a family in Forfar, cathedral people, whose two children went to her dancing class and had a Nanny.

She had been rather looking forward to it and went off happily with her suitcase and Eddy and Christina. The nursery at the top of the large house had bars on the window. They spent a lot of time in the nursery.

It was not that anyone was unkind, at least not deliberately, and the routine was not all that much different from home. The same rules, much the same sort of food, the same bedtime, quite good stories. The same but different. The difference was you couldn't argue. You couldn't say 'I don't want to,' or 'It's not fair', or 'Why can't I...?' If you argued or fought too much at home you were sent straight to bed with no books or toys. Those were the rules. If you argued in this strange

88

nursery you were ignored or excused because you were thought to have been badly brought up. She cried a lot.

She was due to go to Shanwell on the day before her birthday. No one told her the plans had been changed. All morning she waited, sick with excitement, but Nanny did not attempt to pack her clothes. 'Am I going yet?' she asked a dozen times. 'How many times do I have to say it, no,' she was told a dozen times with no explanations. In the end she couldn't stand it. She was trapped forever in this prison with bars. She began to cry, loudly, hysterically, and found she could not stop. She was put to bed.

The children's mother was summoned. She was not pleased. She sat on the edge of the bed and told her to control herself, but by now the sobs like hiccups were coming from somewhere inside and she could not stop. Next morning the chauffeur drove her all the way to Shanwell and she arrived in time for tea.

Mother and father and Bunty and Florence had just got back too. She burst into tears again as soon as she saw them and they explained that the Orkney ferry had been delayed by bad weather. Mother had spent all the voyage being sick.

Annie was back from her holidays too and had made her a cake with nine candles. That was the year she got the camera. A little box Brownie which took eight black and white photographs with one film.

The visit to Forfar was only a pale reflection of what was still to come.

Chapter Nine

Fears and Food and Treats

There was nothing concrete about her terrors. Robbers, murderers, rapists (she had never heard of rape) disturbed her not in the least. Her fears were of the unknown, the unrecognisable, the unseen. Closed doors terrified her. What unspeakable entity might lurk behind the handle? If angels inhabited her house, so could demons. If you believed in the 'resurrection of the dead' as you repeated so glibly every Sunday morning what if someone long dead had resurrected in the empty drawing room behind the closed door? What if there were so many dead people in heaven that some of them chose to resurrect in the day nursery? Could dead people from hell resurrect too? 'What if...' were the key words that she could not keep out of her mind, when, in winter, she was asked to go upstairs and fetch something from mother's room, or the empty nursery behind the closed door.

Darkness too was terrifying. Darkness was 'the light to lighten' the demons. It was fear of the demons in the darkness behind the closed door that rose like sick in her throat. The only way she could cope was to take it all at a run. Two steps at a time up the stairs, a race for the door, a thrust of the handle and a frantic search for the light switch. Sometimes she thought she had caught a glimpse of something indefinable and unspeakably evil which disappeared with the light.

If she had ever been able to put her fear into words, she would have described it as evil. For it was evil she feared most, insubstantial, invisible, ineffable, unconnected with humanity, nothing to do with lying or cheating, biting and scratching, arguing and disobedience. Yet, at the same time, overwhelmingly recognisable. For evil stank.

Mostly she encountered pure evil in her dreams. It lay behind the closed door in a ruinous castle and it was instantly recognisable by its smell. Feral, foul, fiendish, it was the smell of hell. At the same time it was mesmeric. She could not stop herself from climbing that spiral stair and opening that closed door. Sometimes as she stood on its threshold she was aware that she was dreaming. Her mind had awakened but her body still slept. She tried and tried again to scream, but the noise which came out of her mouth was no more than a muffled groan. Unable to move, her body lay there inert, helpless, paralysed, breathing in that great stinking mass of encroaching evil. It took time and strength to force her body awake, to make her screams heard so that Annie would come to her bedside, usually none too pleased. Sometimes she awoke in time to run through to Annie's bed with the thing that was nothing on her heels.

'Cheese dreams,' Annie called these nightmares. Since she seldom, if ever, ate cheese with her milk and biscuits before bed, that was unlikely to be the cause. Mother put them down to too many fairy stories, especially those from the coloured fairytale books. After a while, she realised for herself they were something to do with sleeping on her back. Curled up into a ball was the safest position. That and never forgetting to implore God in her night prayers not to let her have a bad dream. Even so, the dream of evil persisted, less often as she grew older, but none the less terrifying, throughout her life.

Cheese occasionally made its way to the dining room in the form of macaroni or cheese soufflé, a favourite supper dish when the children grew old enough to have something more substantial than biscuits and milk before bed. Rectory meals, on the whole, were fairly predictable.

Breakfasts included porridge liberally sprinkled with sugar followed by scrambled eggs or kedgeree, or, because father like them, stinky kippers or oatmealy herrings. Quite often a bone stuck in your throat and you had to eat dry bread to dislodge it. She hated kippers and herring.

The roast on Sunday was large enough to provide cold meat on Monday, and the remnants minced for shepherd's pie or rissoles or curried on Tuesday. Wednesday was usually offal, liver and bacon, kidney stew or occasionally, and, unpopularly, sweetbreads for a change. On Thursdays there were chops, pork or lamb, and on Fridays, fish, which usually had bones somewhere. Roast chicken or boiling fowl in a white sauce was always served on Saturday. That was her favourite. There was no fat on chicken, and only large identifiable bones.

Vegetables always included potatoes, mashed with milk and butter, boiled with sprinklings of parsley and roasted on Sunday with the joint. Peas and French beans were popular as was cauliflower in a white sauce. Cabbage less so. Beetroot soused in vinegar was Baby's favourite. When no-one was looking she drank vinegar from the bottle. Yuch! Betty hated vinegar. They were expected to finish their vegetables.

Puddings were always plentiful but not always popular. Junket for example was disgusting. She could not understand why father liked it so much. On the other hand treacle tart, made with proper black treacle, was angel food. Semolina and rhubarb, rice pudding and prunes, tapioca and stewed gooseberries which appeared most days of the week, granted, were good for you, or so mother said. She could not believe in her heart that something so horrible as frogs spawn (for a while she really thought it was) could actually be good for you. Worst of all was rice pudding. She remembered A.A. Milne's poem about Mary Jane and rice pudding and thought he had got it about right. It always seemed to be rice pudding day. Sometimes there was steamed syrup pudding, sometimes queen of puddings, sometimes apple tart and custard, but not often enough.

Tea at four o'clock always included scones in a silver warming dish so that the butter melted into the warm dough. Pancakes were more popular especially with a spoonful of strawberry jam. Cakes varied. Christmas cake was not popular except for the almond icing. Chocolate cake was nicest, but, by far the best part of tea-time cake, was raw. There was always a scramble between the three of them to lick the mixing bowl after Hannah had scraped the eggy mixture into the cake tin. The icing bowl was even better, especially lemon-butter icing. Hannah soon learned, as Annie had learned long ago, to let them take turns at licking the bowl, otherwise one of them would surely whine. 'It's not fair. She had it last time.' When it came to treats, they watched each other like hawks.

There were lots of little treats throughout the year like picnics in summer, and, in winter, the *Children's Theatre* whenever it came to Dundee. Bertha Waddell wearing a poked bonnet peeped through the curtain and announced 'Item Number One. Cuckoo! Cuckoo!' Then the curtain swished back and the children would sit entranced as a nursery rhyme or fairy story was sung or acted on the stage.

Once, as a special treat, father took her on her own to see *A Midsummer Night's Dream* by the Dundee Repertory Company. It was decidedly embarrassing because there were not many people in the audience and father laughed so loudly at the antics of Bottom that people turned round and stared at them. Even the actors on the stage were aware of him and played up to his enjoyment.

Father and Mother had a great admiration for the Royal Family. They broke off from opening presents on Christmas afternoon to gather together with Hannah and Annie round the wireless in the drawing-room to listen to the King's annual broadcast. Father listened with tears in his eyes as the new King battled with his stammer. She too agonised over the long pauses as he struggled to speak the words.

The whole family always stood up for the National Anthem whenever they heard it, even in the drawing-room. She was particularly fond of Princess Elizabeth. They were almost the same age (she was four months younger) and they shared the same name. She would much rather have been called Lilibet than Betty, but she kept that to herself.

On one magical occasion they all drove to Edinburgh to see the Royal Family who were due to process down Princess Street for some reason she never knew. On this particular day they stood with the rest of the crowds at the west end of Princess Street clutching small Union Jacks and watched in awe as the open carriage with its mounted escort rolled past. Awestruck, they gazed at the two little girls in straw bonnets with rosebuds round the rim exactly the same as theirs, chatting and laughing together and waving to the crowd. She felt proud, a strange feeling, a cross between crying and laughter which struggled at the back of her throat, and brought tears to her eyes as she waved back.

Once when father and mother were driving them home from a dancing-class at Forfar, they passed a large important-looking car. Father, in the passenger seat, raised his hat and bowed his head and the bearded man in the back seat of the other car who had no hat, also bowed. Father explained that the man in the other car was Lord Strathmore, the Earl of Glamis. 'He's not only the Princesses' grandfather but also a loyal Episcopalian.'

A much-coveted summer treat could only happen when the car roof was lowered. You stood between the legs of the front passenger and poked your head up into the air above the windscreen. It was heavenly sensation, better even than standing on the running board all the way up the East Avenue at Shanwell. The wind tried to blow your hair off and nearly blew your eyes out so you had to screw them up tightly to keep them safe. You had to keep your mouth shut too otherwise you might catch a fly. Sometimes when the wind was really cold, you got earache, but they all three reckoned it was worth it. Turns and times were very strictly kept, (five minutes each go) otherwise there might be sulks or tantrums or massive arguments.

Perhaps the biggest treat of her childhood was a visit to the Glasgow Exhibition of 1936. They went by rail which was a huge treat in itself because it was the first time they had ever been in a train. They darted from side to side of the carriage, raced up and down the corridor and poked their heads out of the window in spite of the warning signs.

It was a sunny day and they ran from one Exhibition Room to another. She liked the Japanese one best. There was a Japanese lady there dressed in a kimono and big sash at the back which mother called an obi. She had a white face and very red lips and she was tiny and beautiful. Betty could not take her eyes off her.

Then, joy of joys, they all rode on the Scenic Railway, a roller-coaster of a ride which was both terrifying and exhilarating as it swung round corners and plunged and soared on its narrow rails. She opened her mouth to scream, but, because everyone else was screaming so loudly, she could not hear herself, so she shouted herself hoarse.

After a scrumptious tea with ice-cream and bought cake, mother wanted to pay a last visit to the India Room. She had been born in India and certainly it was very splendid. It was there that Betty noticed that she had a stiff neck. It was so painful that she could not move her head. Mother wove her scarf round it and after a while it wore off a bit. Her memories of that treat were somewhat overshadowed by the thought of that pain, which no doubt had been caused by the railway ride. From then on, stiff necks were to become a feature of her childhood.

Chapter Ten

Double Figures

That winter was particularly cold. They all had chilblains on their fingers and toes and Jack Frost left elaborate patterns on the windows. Suthy got another cold so they spent long days out in the garden making snowmen and slides on the flagstones outside the study window or sledging in the park. Kirkwood had made her a sledge years before and painted it green. It was extremely heavy but worked well if the hill was steep enough and the snow not too slushy. Bunty had been given a luge which was light and enviable and Baby had a black tin tea tray, which was not much good.

Mother dug out her old skates, elegant and narrow, which fitted Betty with an extra pair of socks. She bought stout new ones for Bunty and Baby had the sort you screwed on to a pair of shoes. With chains on the car tyres, she drove the children up into the Sidlaw Hills to a little round loch which had frozen hard, and, after a lot of stumbling and screaming 'Look at me! Look at me!' they gradually learned to stay upright for at least half a minute on the ice. 'Can we come again tomorrow?' they pleaded as they drove away under darkening skies.

By the time Suthy was well again they could almost skate.

The following winter they went to Shanwell for a couple of weeks after Christmas and there was enough snow and ice that year to satisfy the highest expectations. So many snowy days in the past had fizzled out by the afternoon. They spent the mornings sledging down the Hurlers and in the afternoons trailed all the way up to Golland to a pond in the hills that had frozen over taking it in turns to be pulled by Annie on their sledges.

Horrors! Her skates which had been too big for her last year were now almost too small. Determined to carry on, she crammed her feet into them and staggered on to the ice. The skating was lovely but her feet became numb. That was the year Loch Leven froze into a wonderful wilderness of empty ice. She began to do figures of eight and twirls, but here was a strange thing. She could only skate properly with her right foot. She was as useless with her left foot as with her left hand. Bunty managed to do it with both feet, hands behind her back, pushing to the left, right, left, right, gliding skilfully far out into the distance towards the Castle Island. Mother grew frantic 'It's not safe!' she cried and Betty could see that there were ducks holes all around but Bunty was away in a dream world of her own. 'Stop her! Tell her to come back.' They all shouted and eventually she heard and reluctantly turned round.

They did not go back to Loch Leven. Nor did she mind all that much. The pain of the tight skates had taken the edge off the intense enjoyment of flying through the pale sunlit frosty air.

Back in Dundee it thawed, Suthy recovered enough to return, though she never lost her cough, a hacking destructive explosion which doubled her up and left her shaking and breathless. Father too seemed better, although, as Lent gave way to Easter, he grew quieter, more remote, more anxious. After Easter he was ordered complete rest. One of the cathedral families, jute millionaires who lived in a big house on the outskirts of Dundee, took him under their wing, but he was as homesick for his family as they were for him.

Mother did her best to keep them busy. She bought a sampler for Betty to sew in cross-stitch. It had Edward XIIIth name and coat-of-arms and 1937 on it, but Edward had abdicated in favour of his brother George by this time so mother told her that it was 'a piece of history' and she must finish it. She hated it because most of the time she spent unpicking wrong stitches and there were little dots of blood where she pricked her finger. Mother had it properly stretched and framed and fortunately you couldn't see the blood.

She entered Betty and Bunty for a Children's Hour competition for the best-dressed dolls which were to go to a Children's Hospital. Mother and Suthy and Annie did most of the stitching and knitting required so it was hardly surprising that they both won prizes. Her prize was a little book about Joan of Arc.

On some Sunday nights when Annie and Hannah were out, they invaded the kitchen and mother made toffee. She boiled soft brown sugar, butter and milk together and poured it out into a huge oval willow-pattern ashette. It was supposed to last all week, but most of it was consumed when still soft and warm. It never turned out the same twice running. Sometimes it was as hard as a brick, sometimes soft and runny, sometimes sugary, sometimes smooth. No matter. It always tasted delicious.

99

On other nights they played board games. Her favourite was *Knight's Quest*. Six knights set out to rescue a beautiful princess who lay on a sofa enmeshed in a bower of enchanted roses. The hazards were many and exciting. The Red Knight got trapped in a dragon's den; throw a six to continue. The Yellow Knight was enchanted by an evil witch; miss a turn. The Green Knight got lost in a thicket of roses; move backwards for three turns. (That was when you always threw sixes.) They played *Ludo* and *Halma* and *Chinese Chequers* too but *Knight's Quest* was by far the favourite and often went on well beyond bedtime.

Pocket money went up that year. It was now 6d instead of 3d and mostly you spent it in the paper shop. You walked down Blackness Avenue for a short distance, then up Hyndford Street and then down Blackness Road where the trams hurtled past until you came to the shop. Mother used to take the children there first thing on Saturday mornings when she went to pay the paper bill or buy odds and ends like matches or birthday cake candles and they would spend ages deciding whether to buy liquorice straps or conversation lozenges, or, at great expense, a 2d bar of chocolate.

Betty was in double figures now so was allowed to go to the paper shop by herself or with Bunty. Sometimes mother would ask her to get cigarettes. 'Just tell them to put it down,' she said and no money exchanged hands. 'Put it down,' were magic words. It worked for chocolate and 'soor plooms' and acid drops too. Mother discovered this at the end of the month when the bill came in. She was cross because, although Betty denied it hotly, she knew perfectly well that she had done wrong. However the result in the long run was good. Pocket money went up.

So did her weekly expenses. That was the year the *Beano* and the *Dandy* made their first appearance. At 2d each, she and Bunty shared the comic books. Korky the Kat, Beryl the Peril, Lord Haw Haw, Desperate Dan, Dennis the Menace became household personalities in the same way that the Broons and Oor Wullie from the *Sunday Post* enlivened Sunday afternoons in the kitchen.

That was also the year of Torty. Cats had never featured highly in a household that was devoted to dogs. There had never been a cat in Dundee but that summer she had seen a litter of kittens on the hearth at Shanwell farm and when Mrs Forrester told her she could take her pick, she wanted the scruffy little tortoiseshell runt with a desperation that mother and father could not deny. 'You'll have to look after him,' they warned her. 'I will. I promise I will,' she assured them almost too excited to breathe. 'You can't take him to Dundee,' mother said. 'It wouldn't be fair. He's a country cat, poor creature.'

When the holidays ended there was no thought of leaving Torty behind. He went everywhere with her, and slept on her pillow. She dressed him up in her dolls' clothes, put him in the pram and took him for walks, played endlessly with him until her wrists were a tapestry of scratches. 'You'll maul him to death,' mother warned but he thrived. Everyone loved Torty. He even managed not to upset Tigger too much. He tolerated Dundee but he was happiest at Shanwell where he hunted for rabbits and mice, and, she did not like to think too much about this, he also caught birds.

Hunting was his downfall, or so it was assumed. Mr Kirkwood had traps everywhere. He went out one day and never came back. They all searched for the rest of the holidays. She made herself ill with weeping but he was never found.

Chapter Eleven

Illness

Like a dark cloud, illness spread its shadow across her childhood. It began with mother. Baby was scarcely a year old when she became gravely ill, so ill that she had to have an operation. Betty had no idea what an operation was but she knew it was serious. Later she discovered that it was to remove her thyroid gland. In those days that operation was life-threatening and indeed she grew to understand that mother's life had hung in the balance for three days.

She was not ill at home. Dee Dundas in Stirling, as usual, came to the rescue, took her in, cosseted and tried to divert her, then drove her to Perth Infirmary where she was to remain for three weeks before returning to Stirling to recuperate. In all she was away about three months.

Three months without seeing her children, without them seeing her, was a lifetime for all of them. She missed Baby's first birthday and Bunty's third, the busy happy continuity of family life. No wonder, as father said, she felt dreich.

Father and Annie between them managed. He read them stories, heard their prayers and had meals with them when he could. There was only one small disaster. He had been holding a cup of hot tea. Somehow Betty managed to joggle his arm and upset the cup. A big splash fell on the instep of her right foot. She screamed with pain. Father bent down to take off her sock and there was a round penny-worth of scarlet skin that was already trying to blister. Father blamed himself but as Annie pointed out tartly she had been told over and over again to sit still at meal times. It was her own fault.

Father brought in a recruit, his niece Alison, their first cousin, who was in her twenties, to help with the children. Alison had a round face with glasses and she did her serious best to take mother's place. She played games with them, read to them and took them for no-dawdling walks in the park when Annie was busy, and genuinely tried to be helpful. She had been brought up by a nanny who still lived with her family and she was rather fond of saying, 'Nanny wouldn't approve of elbows on the table', or 'Nanny doesn't allow children to speak with their mouths full', and 'Nanny doesn't like little girls who answer back'. That was said after the big row.

Betty couldn't abide fat. Every scrap had to be cut off the Sunday roast or the midweek chops, every strip off the breakfast bacon. It had been accepted in the family a long time ago that Betty was allowed to leave her fat. Alison, however, did not know this. 'Nanny expected little girls to eat every scrap on the plate, including the fat.'

Betty answered back. 'Mummy doesn't,' she said triumphantly. It was true. Mother could not bear to eat fat either. Father was not there to make the peace so Betty sat sullenly in front of the congealing fat on her plate until Hannah came in to clear the plates.

'Miss Betty has not finished yet,' Alison said crisply.

'I have,' she said loudly. By now she was in a really bad mood and so was Hannah who had strong labour leanings. 'Miss Betty' indeed! Betty was only 'missed' by the Kirkwoods who belonged to the 'old school'.

That was when Alison said, 'Nanny doesn't approve of little girls who answer back.'

'I don't have to eat fat, do I?' she appealed to Bunty, but Bunty whom Alison had already chided for crying when she lost at *Beggar my Neighbour,* pretended not to hear.

'Do I?' she appealed to Hannah who, already riled, said, 'I'll bring your pudding, pet.'

'No pudding, I'm afraid, until she finishes her fat,' Alison said firmly

She sat there stony-faced while the others in virtuous silence ate stewed rhubarb and semolina. She was still sitting there when Alison told the others they might say their grace and leave the table.

'Thank-you-God-for-my-good-food-please-may-I-get-down,' Bunty and Baby gabbled and slid off their seats to escape to the nursery.

'It's up to you,' Alison said, not unkindly, ignoring the tears of mortification that had begun to slide down Betty's cheeks. 'Finish your plate and you can join us.'

She folded her napkin, shut her eyes for a moment no doubt saying her own grace and left the room.

'It's not fair,' she told Hannah when she came in to clear the table.

'Just eat it, pet,' Hannah advised whipping away the other plates and glasses and piling them on a tray.

By now the fat had congealed into white strips and the gravy had separated. 'I'll be sick,' she threatened. She got as far as putting a lump on to her fork and lifting it to her mouth. 'I just can't, 'she whined.

But by now Hannah had left the dining-room.

Betty was still there when father returned. He was saddened rather than angry as he listened to her tearful excuses but he didn't let her off. 'Your cousin has come a long way to look after you. She is trying very hard to bring you up properly while Mummy is ill and you have been singularly unhelpful.' She was sobbing by now. 'You have a choice,' he told her gently. 'Finish your food or bed.'

Still sobbing she slipped from her chair and threw herself into his arms. Bed it would have to be. 'I'm sorry, I'm sorry, I'm sorry,' she sobbed.

He held her close and kissed her. 'I know you are. Now you need to tell Alison.'

She had never missed mother more than at that moment. In bed there, as always, was her blanket.

The children ran through the list of childhood diseases. Whooping cough, measles, coughs and colds. Father had a cure for colds which was particularly repulsive. Quinine. At the sign of a snuffle they had to endure a spoonful of the bitter, hateful, colourless liquid. He told them he had regularly dosed his choirboys in Aberdeen and it always worked. None of them ever caught cold. Or perhaps they just didn't tell him, she wondered, but she kept that thought to herself. Mother's cure-all was cod-liver oil malt which was just about bearable, though it left a nasty aftertaste, but Virol malt in its dark brown bottle was a daily treat that they all looked forward to.

On one occasion she had really enjoyed being ill. She had woken one morning feeling a bit odd, got up, taken off her nightie and caught a glimpse of herself in the mirror. She was covered in spots, nasty, itchy pimples all over her tummy, her legs and her arms. The Pill was sent for and chicken pox diagnosed.

There were two theories. Mix freely with the others so that they all caught it at once, or keep her quarantined for three weeks and hope no one else caught it. Gerald's mother made a fuss so her mother had to make the latter decision. Betty moved into the spare room where she had meals by herself. Suthy, who had had chicken pox when she was young, gave her separate lessons in the spare room. She even went for walks by herself, trailing behind Suthy or Annie and her sisters at a suitable distance. To cheer her up, mother drove her down town when she went shopping and they bought new jumpers for all three of them at Draffens, knee-length socks at D M Brown and fish at Cantrell's. It was the greatest time, because, although she felt spoilt and special, she never felt the least bit ill, only a little itchy.

But not all illnesses were so benign. Certainly not father's which caused numbness sometimes in his arms and legs, sometimes in his face, made him exhausted and depressed and threatened his heart so that he had to spend long periods in bed or recuperating out of the parish. It puzzled the Pill who even visited him at Shanwell bringing with him one specialist after another. Some alleviation came after one of these specialists diagnosed a rare blood disease with an unpronounceable name in which the blood grew too thick to travel easily through the arteries. He prescribed leeches. Some substance in the leech's bite helped to thin the blood.

What a dreadful cure. She could barely bring herself to think of it. She would gladly have taken quinine every night to save her father from such a punishment. The chemist himself brought the white box and together with the Pill they did what they had to do. She never knew how many leeches they brought. Hopefully it was only one. It helped him for a little while at the time but not in the long run.

Father and mother kept cheerful with the children but they were not blind. They could see the anxious faces, overhear snatches of conversation, kitchen gossip, all of which begged the same question. Would father ever get better? If not, should he retire and leave the work he loved? If so, where would they go?

One day the tension lifted. Mother was smiling, father his old teasing self. Mother told her that father had been offered by Dean Don a grace and favour flat in Hampton Court in exchange for light duties. They might be moving to London, but by the end of the week father was ill again and they both knew that even this would be too much. The offer was reluctantly declined.

With father's health so uncertain, no one properly noticed Suthy. Her father, the elderly professor, had died and that was sad. After a week she returned and lessons continued much as before. She grew thinner, she coughed a lot, nor did her eyes shine and she practically stopped smiling. One morning she left the children to write a story about King Alfred burning the cakes because she wanted to talk privately to mother. When they both came back into the nursery, Betty noticed that Suthy had been crying. She was still crying while mother explained that this would be her last day because Helen was not very well and the doctor had said she had to go abroad for her health, South Africa, in fact, to live with her sister.

There was no more work done that day. Suthy did not even stay for lunch. She was too upset. They were all too upset. When mother drove her down to the ferry, Betty had wanted to go too, but the way mother said 'no' warned her not to argue and she had looked preoccupied and worried when she came back.

'Is that serious?' Betty had asked. 'Will she get better in South Africa?'

'I hope so,' mother had said without much hope in her voice.

She never saw her again.

Chapter Twelve

Here and There
Here and there. One small alphabet letter. All it took was a 't' to encompass the difference between home and school. At the beginning she would have gone so far as to say heaven and hell, but even then she knew that wasn't true for home was not exactly heaven at that time and school was not quite hell.

With Suthy gone in the middle of February, decisions had to be made and made quickly. Another governess would have to be found but Betty was getting too old for governesses and there was a private school down the hill that had been recommended called Seymour Lodge.

Father had wanted them all to go to East Grinstead where the Sisters of St Margaret of Antioch, a community founded by his grandfather, John Mason Neale, ran a girls' boarding school to which all the cousins, including Alison, had gone. But it was 1938 and if, as was likely, there was another war, Sussex was not the ideal situation for children. Meanwhile a temporary governess was found, a pretty young woman with abundant corn-gold hair and surprisingly strict, to see the term out.

Betty was in no way involved in the final decision so it came as a complete shock to her when mother and father told her that on May 4 she was going to St Katharine's, a junior boarding school in St Andrews.

She could not remember being so excited. Lately her reading had included the *Chalet School* series and she had recently discovered a black and yellow paper-covered magazine called *Schoolgirl's Own* which she greedily devoured. There was nothing she wanted so much as to go to boarding school. She was ecstatic.

One day mother drove her by herself to Forsyth's in Princes Street, Edinburgh, to buy the uniform. She had never seen so many clothes. Six pairs of navy knickers, six pairs of knicker linings, six pairs of lisle stockings, six pairs of short lisle socks as it was the summer term, walking shoes, house shoes, gym shoes, tennis shoes, cotton frocks, overalls, overcoat, hats, berets, skirts, shirts, a tie in the house colours. The list seemed endless and she also needed a trunk to pack it in.

She hung everything carefully in the wardrobe in the spare room and gave everyone who called at the Rectory

109

a guided tour of her 'trousseau', as Sister Grace called it. She was sent presents too, a little travelling clock in a morocco red case from Uncle Bob and Aunt Nell, a photograph frame from Auntie Maimie, a spongebag from Pam across the road, a tooled leather writing case from Auntie Sine which she had made herself with writing-paper and envelopes, a pocket-sized New Testament with pictures by Margaret Tarrant from father and mother. It was like having another birthday. Excitement jiggled around inside her increasing as the days flew past.

Nobody thought to warn her. She had no inkling of how it would be until she was in the car, dressed up in her new uniform with mother and father and Bunty and Baby all there to take her to St Kay's. She had not known how it would feel when mother and father and her sisters drove away without her. Her father had blessed her and wept.

Home-sickness is not just a state of mind. It has a unique physical manifestation, a raw, yearning, yawning, hungry emptiness that starts somewhere in the gut and affects the whole body. It engulfed her in that moment and would continue to swamp her from time to time throughout the remainder of her life.

Those first few weeks were spent in a welter of tears. She could not look at her photographs arranged on her small dressing table without crying. When, for breakfast, she was presented with fried bread and fried tomatoes, a fruit she loathed, she cried. When she knelt down beside her narrow little bed in the dormitory she shared with five other girls, she cried. Sometimes Miss West, the genial housemistress, took her downstairs to her drawing-room and tried to cheer her up with cocoa and kindly chat, but still she cried. Suddenly, if in the middle of an English lesson if the word 'mother' appeared in the text, she cried. Her first letter home written on her new notepaper in the tooled leather case was blotched with tears. She wrote to everyone, her sisters, Annie, Hannah, the Kirkwoods, Pam, even Tigger, by now an evil-tempered adult dog, and she cried her way through all of them.

At St Kay's the girls each had a number. This was called House Order and your position depended on your age and behaviour. Because she was the only new girl that summer term, her place was right at the bottom, thirty-sixth. This meant that anyone who was above you, even one place, could report you to Miss West. Everyone reported her for crying, even number thirty-five who was also called Betty and who was to become her best friend.

'Please Miss West, or Miss Duguid (the housekeeper), or Matron (whom the girls thought was a German spy) Betty's crying again.'

For about three weeks there was scarcely an hour went by without tears. Then one day Betty Mair said generously, 'Would you like to play chuckies?'

Chuckies was all the fashion, just as yo-yos had been a year or so back. You chucked up a handful of marbles and tried to catch one of them on the back of your hand. Once that feat had been mastered, and it was not easy, you had to catch two and so on until you had five of them balanced precariously on the back of your hand. She never mastered more than one but the trying was fun. There were no tears for at least an hour. Then next day Miss Williams, her English mistress, gave her a VG for her essay. She discovered that she liked Miss Williams,

111

who had a long face, a very long nose and long grey hair in a bun but beautiful grey eyes. At play-time she beat Mary Buist at tennis and then they had stovies for supper. Stovies was made with potatoes and gravy and onions and it was totally delicious. There were no tears at all that day.

She started an elaborate calendar to mark off the days until the Friday of half term. Mother came alone to drive her home. Her sisters were still at school, father was out visiting, Hannah had baked a Victoria sponge. Gradually she felt herself slipping out of her acquired persona of shy, unpopular, teary new-girl and became what she always had been, bossy eldest sister, confident eldest daughter, who thought she knew everything, who knew that she was beloved.

There had been a new acquisition to the family, a thin, crooked, intense-eyed man of indeterminate age called Lance. It was an open secret that he had been in prison and father, taking pity on him, had offered him a job as gardener. In return, he worshipped the family and was always bringing little gifts, including two enormous shop-made birthday cakes for her sisters which caused her small twinges of jealousy. Shop-bought cakes were a luxury indeed. One had green icing with pink sugar rosebuds.

'He sounds nice' she said, as they drove on to the Dundee ferry.

'He tries hard to please everyone,' mother answered, 'but I can hardly fault him for that.'

'Why was he in prison?' she asked, but mother didn't know. 'Father says he's a reformed character.'

She changed the subject. 'We thought you should have a room to yourself so we've moved you to the spare room. I hope you agree.'

The room to herself gave her mixed feelings, part pride, that now she really was old enough to have a room to herself, part humiliation. Was she now a guest in her own home? It occurred to her that everything in life had a good and a bad side. Being treated as a grown-up was good. Why then was she suddenly swamped by those dreadfully familiar homesick pangs? The nearer she got to home, the more she longed for what she had been but could never be again, for the life that had once been hers, but had gone forever. That Sunday morning father preached about Eve and the Tree of Knowledge. She knew exactly what he was talking about. Did Eve, too, long for the bliss of ignorance? As the hours wore on she knew that, in spite of her own room, her home life had not changed, but she had, irrevocably, irretrievably, eternally.

Her sisters were polite for about ten minutes. After tea they played *Monopoly* and squabbled as usual. She was allowed to go to bed at nine and on Sunday after church they drove over to Shanwell for one short glorious summer night. Monday was haunted by the threat of going back to school. She started crying at breakfast and carried on intermittently all day soaking three handkerchiefs. When father hugged her she thought her heart would break.

But pulling on her school persona was not as hard as it had been the first time. There were bad moments like when Mrs Webster got angry with her for not knowing how to parse. Grammar had not been part of Suthy's curriculum. Nor Latin either, but her class mates were not that far ahead and she soon learned to catch up. No copy-book script, so she was told her handwriting looked as if a spider had climbed out of the ink-well. Everyone else in the class laughed, but it was not funny. On the other hand she was well ahead in English and basked in glory when her poem called *The Plough* was read out and everyone clapped. And there were other good moments like swimming in the icy pool carved out of the North Sea, summer Saturday picnics to a local farm and Guides.

Chapter Thirteen

Guides, Stealing and the Family Way

When the chance came to join the Girl Guides, Betty took it to her heart, body and soul. Not that she was ever a particularly good Guide. She never reached the elevated ranks of patrol leader with one or two white stripes on her pocket, but that was not to be expected. She had joined the St Katharine's Company after everyone else and was happy just to be a member of the Bluebell Patrol. She learned the Guide Law, practised the three-fingered salute and made her solemn promises in front of the whole company to the Captain, Miss Lindsay, who taught Scripture.

Although her ambition was to have a sleeve full of badges, she managed to earn only two, one for First Aid and the other came out of the blue from the art teacher who issued them to the whole class for lino cuts. She polished her brooch till it shone, learned how to fold and tie the orange cloth around her neck and attached a knife with gadgets and a whistle to her leather belt. She loved Guides so devotedly that she even sacrificed one of her precious holiday weeks to go to camp.

It started on the last day of term. They changed into their navy-blue Guide tunics, packed their overnight cases with exciting new gadgets, a tin mug, a knife, fork and spoon neatly slotted together, a sleeping bag and a roll of lavatory paper. Lavatory paper? That made them giggle as they trooped in an orderly, Guiderly way into the bus. Everything they did was orderly and Guiderly. The tents, big, conical and canvas were large enough for the six girls of a patrol to sleep together, toes to the middle pole. Every morning the flaps round the bottom of the tent were raised and every night while they slept, they were lowered. The Patrols took it in turn to dig the latrines, light the fires, carry wood, clear away the dead ash, cook the meals and organise the evening campfire sing-songs.

During the days, there were outings first to a nearby dairy farm, then the Lomond Hills, to a boating loch and finally to a paper mill owned by the father of one of the Guides. She did not like to think about the paper mill.

In the middle of a huge shed there was a conical pile of old papers as big as a tent waiting to be re-pulped. Most of the papers were women's magazines and comic books. She saw *Peoples' Friends, Beanos, Dandy's, Rovers*, and, joy of joy, the yellow and black cover of a *Schoolgirl's Own*. The mill owner was beaming at them. 'Please, girls, help yourselves. There must be something here you haven't read.'

115

Miss Lindsay made a thank-you speech, then turned to the eager Guides. 'You may take one comic each, one only, remember.'

She pounced on the copy she had noticed. No, she hadn't read it, then she found another and yet another. Which to choose? Miss Lindsay blew her whistle. That meant 'stop what you're doing and come here at once'. The Guides scrambled to obey. No one was paying Betty any attention. Quickly she stuffed one copy into the front of her tunic, and, holding the other ostentatiously aloft, ran to join the others.

No one noticed the small bulk under her tunic, but during the rest of the tour, the picnic lunch provided by the owner's wife and the bus ride home, she was conscious of its unsettling presence. Undressing that night, she managed to slip it deep inside the folds of her sleeping bag, while ostentatiously brandishing the legitimate copy. But here was a strange thing. She found it deeply boring.

Soon it grew too dark to read but she could not sleep. She slipped on her coat, and, after informing the patrol leader that she was going to the 'aunt' (school name for the latrines), she crossed the campsite as the stars were beginning to come out. Miss Lindsay's tent was smaller, cottage-shaped and she had a lamp. As Betty passed she saw that she was still in uniform and on her knees beside her low camp bed, her back straight as poker and her hands folded in prayer.

She ran to the latrines and burst into tears.

She meant to own up but next morning they were woken at six. It was time to strike camp, pack up and catch the bus back to school where their parents were waiting to take them home for the long summer holidays.

Yes, she enthused to mother, she had had a wonderful time, yes, the weather had been dry most of the time, yes, it had been great fun, but, somehow, after that, Guiding lost its magic. She never went back.

So was she a thief? There had been other little incidents.

One of the pieces of furniture in the drawing-room was a Jacobean court chest, full of cupboards and drawers. Mother kept the family sweets in a large square biscuit tin in one of the upper cupboards. These could be chocolates left over from Christmas or Easter, toffees in coloured wrapping paper, barley sugar, (not popular) or fruit drops dusted in icing sugar which, from time to time, mother bought. Every day after lunch they were allowed to choose two sweets each. It was best to take boiled sweets because they lasted longest and to avoid the rich chocolates because they nearly always had nuts in them and had to be spat out. Replacements were not allowed.

The children were seldom alone in the drawing room until Betty started to have piano lessons. Everyday while Suthy was busy with the younger children she spent half-an-hour practising alone and every day the cupboard loomed larger. No-one would know, no-one would see, no-one would ever find out if she took just one. For days she resisted, but the temptation grew too strong. To begin with it was strictly one, a toffee hastily chewed while she thumped out her scales. Then it was two. One day it was three. Did she really think no one would notice? Certainly no one said anything but one day when she went straight to the cupboard, she found that the sweets

117

had gone. Maybe mother was just rearranging things the way she sometimes did because nothing was ever said. After lunch that day when the cupboard was usually opened, mother told them she had decided to keep the tin in her room. No reason was given, and, strangely enough, no questions were asked, but she felt herself grow scarlet all over. It never occurred to her that she might not be the only one in the household to visit the Jacobean court-chest.

That was not the only sneaky thing that she was ashamed of. *Gone with the Wind* was a book all the grown-ups were talking about. One day she overheard mother chatting to Mrs Guild on the telephone. She was only half listening but when she overheard her mother say. 'Of course it's not a book to leave lying about for obvious reasons' she was intrigued. Mrs Guild then said something which made mother laugh and the subject was changed, but Betty had heard enough. She was consumed with curiosity.

Mother usually left her Boots Library books on a small table beside her chair in the drawing room, but the book was not there. It was not hard to guess where it would be. Things that her parents did not want her or her sisters to meddle with were kept in the study in one of the four large glass-fronted expandable bookcases. The study itself was quiet and private when father was there saying his 'words' or writing his sermons and you were expected to knock quietly and not go bursting in. When the door was closed you knew father would be there but when it was open, she often sneaked in to read in peace or to write her poems.

Gone with the Wind was not hard to find. It was a huge book, with a blue cover and she spotted it straight away in the first of the bookcases lying sideways above the Anthony Trollopes. She took it out and started reading. She had never read anything like it. Utterly absorbed, she took every opportunity to snatch a chapter. Try though she might she could not discover what made the book so unsuitable. Perhaps it was the word 'pregnant'. She knew what it meant but it was not a word her parents used, too explicit perhaps, almost rude. Mother used the word *enceinte* and Annie and Hannah spoke of being 'in the family way'. One of Annie's sisters was in the family way. Then one day the book wasn't there. Mother had taken it back to the library so she never got the chance to find out what was so bad about it.

She had known about 'being in the family way' for most of her life for mother had made no secret of the fact that when she was expecting first Bunty and then Baby. When she was little she would strut around pushing her middle out as far as possible and boast to anyone who would listen that she had a baby in her tummy. But then she forgot until one day on a walk in the park she saw a woman with the most enormous stomach. Shocked and appalled, her first thought was that the woman must have some terrible illness. She could not take her eyes off her. Annie told her sharply not to stare but refused to speculate as to what might be wrong with the woman. Betty realised that Annie was embarrassed and immediately she had felt embarrassed too. It was only afterwards when she read *Gone with the Wind* that she associated the word pregnant with something indecent. She never did finish the book.

Chapter Fourteen

Summer Hols

After a year at boarding school, home was not the same. There were of course the obvious changes; war on the horizon, Father very frail, Bunty and Baby now going to the High School because Seymour Lodge had moved to the country, Hannah gone, married and not replaced. But the main difference was in herself. She was three people and she didn't much care for at least two of them. The schoolgirl on the verge of adolescence, was giggly, unconfident, craved popularity and friendship, untidy with a pile of dormitory marks to prove it, clumsy at netball, hopeless at gym (she couldn't somersault), sloppy in the class room, not particularly good at anything - that VG for English was seldom repeated.

The daughter-at-home could not have been more different. Sometimes she stood outside herself and wondered despairingly who exactly was this rude, moody, lazy, superior person that she had become.

The third person first appeared a couple of mornings after the beginning of the summer holidays at Shanwell. She had awoken early to a perfect July morning, lushly green, noisy with birdsong, flooded with sunshine. Instead of turning over and going back to sleep she got up, dressed and unlocked the front door. No one else was about. She had the world to herself, and what a world it was! Following the path through the trees down to the Wee House, sadly neglected and growing toadstools inside, she began to run along the tennis walk beside the paddock, through the Spanish chestnut wood, between clumps of ragged robin, nettles and wild cicely, over the stile, across the road and up the High Planting. The rooks were cawing in the tall pines, the sun shone in long shafts of light between the trees, her body felt light and strong, her mind was at peace, her whole being suffused with joy. She began to sing, bits of the *Mikado* which they were doing at school, songs they had learned with Suthy, 'Summer is a-comin' in, loudly sing cuckoo!' and 'Annie Laurie'. She shouted them at the top of her voice until she reached the pool by the water-gate. She did not think twice but stripped off her cotton dress and knickers and plunged into the deepest part. The cold took her breath away and after half a second she emerged glistening, freezing yet on fire with joy.

She stayed that person all morning, bicycling uncomplainingly with Bunty to pick up the daily messages in Kinross, but then at lunchtime mother asked her if she would help dead-head the roses that afternoon and she felt herself slip back into the moody, supercilious persona and there was nothing she could do to stop the grey blanket of discontent swamping her whole self. She answered ungraciously and stalked out of the dining room.

The morning bathe became a routine, rain or shine. The moods came and went with a hateful frequency. Often after a particularly ugly display of rudeness she would bang out of the house and just walk. And as she walked right up into the hills above Ledlanet, passed Upper Warroch, she would tell herself stories. Sometimes the stories involved Grey Owl, sometime Miss Williams the English teacher, but always she was at the centre, calm, beautiful, beloved, special. She would cover miles following a burn up its lush banks to its source while the stories unfurled against the background music of running water like a many-fronded fern in her head. It was almost like being asleep.

Once she awoke to find herself high up in the hills. There was no sign of human habitation, no scuttering rabbit, no hovering sparrow-hawk or startled grouse, only the humps of half-a-dozen hills under a leaden sky. She had blundered into an alien world. The hills glared down at her, resenting her intrusion. They threatened to crush her. The sky glowered, the heather scratched her bare legs, the wind buffeted her body coldly. She knew she was not wanted here.

Terrified, she began to run downhill so fast that it felt as if she might start to fly. Instead she tripped over a hidden boulder and fell flat on her face knocking the breath out of her body. As she sat up gasping for air, she could see below her the whole beautiful panorama of Fife turning golden with the promise of an early harvest. For no reason that she could understand, she began to cry.

A week later and the harvest cutting began. She and her sisters were there to help stook the sheaves as they fell, bound in string, from the binder. Wet and thistly, the bundles of oats, wheat or barley were bunched into little cottages of eight. Everyone including Annie came out to help, rain or shine, and at noon young Mrs Forrester arrived with doorstep cheese sandwiches and an urn of strong hot sweet tea. Betty was so thirsty, she was glad to drink even tea. .

After the stooking, if the weather was dry, came the lifting. This year she was promoted to the top of a cart while Bunty stood on the tractor brake between each little clump. She quickly learned to pull the sheaf off the pitch fork and arrange it so that the cartload grew higher and higher. The best bit was lying flat on top of the fragrant sheaves as the tractor trundled the load back to the stackyard then hurling the sheaves down to the stackers. Barley ears stuck into their clothing, thistles scratched their fingers and she was too tired for moods. When it was time to go back to school, although there were often still sodden stooks standing in the fields, Sam or Jimmy Forrester always gave them a precious pound each, but they would gladly have done it for nothing.

At school she had long ago devised an escape from her unconfident uncomfortable school persona. It happened during the day whenever she had a free period or during the evening hour of preparation before drawing-room. She would hurry through her school work (little wonder her exercise books were scarred with red ink correction marks and dubbed 'careless'), get out her red notebook and scribble verse after verse of poetry. What she enjoyed most was the editing and she would spend hours experimenting with the right word, the best rhyme or the proper rhythm. Sometimes she showed her poems to Miss Williams who was always encouraging, always interested and often had a suggestion to make. That way she became another person. That way she was happy.

Chapter Fifteen

War and St Leonards

She often wondered about being grown-up. How did you change and when? Was it when you were eighteen or twenty-one perhaps? Did you wake up one morning and realise that you were different? When she was small she wanted to be a missionary with six children. Now she thought she probably wanted to write best-sellers, because mother, who was into reading best-sellers, planted the idea. She secretly hoped she might become a poet, because there was nothing she enjoyed doing so much as writing poetry. She also knew, because P-P, her new English teacher, more or less said so. 'You get it in Keats, you get it in Rupert Brooke,' she thundered, bonking the desk with her enormous bust. That magical 'it' that made someone a poet was not to be found in Betty.

That August she was thirteen. When father's holiday was over, Mother left Annie in charge of Bunty and Baby and took Betty with father back to Dundee. Hannah, having got married, was no longer with them so mother had said 'You'll be a great help to me, darling.' Was this then what it was like to be grown-up? Certainly she felt different, not exactly exultant but certainly exalted, sitting in the back of the car, waving goodbye to her sisters. Was this then a taste of what was to come? If so it was a good feeling. She almost became what she was expected to be.

All the talk was of war. Mother had already lined the drawing-room curtains with black-out material but the bedrooms were still to finish. On Thursday Hitler's troops entered Danzig. She spent Friday morning with Pam across the road giggling about new neighbours who had a son called John about their age. The following day, Saturday, the police called to fit them with gas masks. She tried hers on and gagged at the rubbery smell which reminded her of the dentist gas. In the case of war, they explained, they were to be carried everywhere at all times. Mother spent most of the day lining curtains.

On Sunday 3 September, having been to the early Communion service, she offered to get lunch ready so that mother could take father back to Matins. He no longer drove in case one of those frightening attacks of numbness caused an accident.

It felt strange being alone in the house, though 'alone' was perhaps not the right word. The building itself seemed alive with a watchful personality of its own, not frightening, though, more friendly and familiar. Shanwell was like that too, older, distinct from, but a little like Auntie Meg. Perhaps all houses had personalities of their own. As she peeled and boiled some potatoes, she thought about the houses she knew and realised that each had its own 'aliveness', perhaps not always good. How awful, she thought, to live in an unkind house.

She arranged the cold ham that mother had left in the larder on a serving plate, cut up the tomatoes from the Shanwell greenhouse and wished for the umpteenth time that she liked their taste because they smelt so good. She found only one slug as she washed the lettuce. That was a record. Usually there were never less than three and once she had counted seven. Then she shelled the broad beans that she herself had picked before they left Shanwell. She loved broad beans but they were tricky. You had to boil them for a little while, then squeeze them out of their little jackets and mix them in a white sauce, but she did not know how to make the sauce so she stirred in some butter instead. There seemed to be very few of them. She laid the table in the dining-room, saw that the napkin rings in the sideboard were tarnished after the long summer and gave them a rub with the silver cloth before fitting each with a clean napkin. She thought, as she waited, her mother and father would be proud of her.

Neither of them noticed. War had been declared at 11 15 during Matins and father had had to tell the congregation. A little later when the air raid siren sounded they listened, appalled, for the sound of aircraft, but the world outside was completely silent. It was the first time she was to hear that sinister wail and then came the all-clear. Lunch conversation was about trivialities, getting Miss Matheson to help line the curtains, buying gas-mask cases to replace the cardboard boxes, when to fetch the family from Shanwell, evacuation, filling the car with petrol before rationing started, stocking up with sugar and tea…but her parents looked stricken.

Next day air raids were expected to start in earnest, but there was nothing. She and mother decided to drive over to Edinburgh as had been planned to buy her new school uniform for she was moving up from St Katharines to Castlecliffe, one of the ten houses that made up St Leonards School in St Andrews. A black silk dress and black silk stockings were required for dancing classes with a white silk dress for Speech Day, two oatmeal tweed skirts, one matching jacket, one long tweed coat, four shirts, two house ties, a gym tunic with a wide canvas belt to which was attached a tail of silk in the house colours (purple and black) for games. She had grown out of all her shoes, and now needed five new pairs which included black lavatory-heeled dancing shoes and galoshes. She needed new underwear, new pyjamas, and, exciting this, a bra, 'B-squared,' as they called it at school, long lisle stockings and a suspender belt. It all amounted to a great deal of money which mother and father could not afford. Fortunately her godfather came to the rescue with a large cheque, and an Orkney friend donated her old cloak, the one item on the clothing list that she liked. The ankle-length, navy blue, serge cloak with the house colours lining the hood was longer and heavier than the modern version and already had two name tapes of previous owners sewn behind the front opening. She loved her cloak.

She was not so confident about big school as she had been about going to St Kays, and she was only a little reassured when everyone told her how much pleasanter it would be. With a heavy heart she helped to sew on her names tapes, and pack all her new clothes in her trunk, which, under the system 'luggage in advance', the railway people called for and delivered a few days later to the school address. It would be there waiting for her in the boot-room with all the other trunks ready to be unpacked.

The following day Mother drove over to Shanwell to pick up Bunty and Florence and Annie. She and Pam went to the swimming baths. If this was war, then what was all the fuss all about?

The worry, of course, was not just war, although that loomed always on the periphery of every difficult decision. Father was no better. He spent long periods between Sundays resting with Dee Dundas or other kindly cathedral people. Money was tight. Father's stipend as provost was £500 a year which was adequate, generous even by church standards, but it was mother's income that paid for the extras, servants, school bills and with the war that had already begun to dwindle dangerously. Where were they to live when father could no longer work? Where were the school fees for three children to come from? Though she was not directly involved in these anxieties because father and mother were careful not to discuss their concerns openly, yet the three children were uneasily aware that all was far from well. It was for these reasons that Betty was not too dreich about returning to school. Her personal concerns were not so dispiriting as father's illness and mother's anxiety.

Bunty and Baby were already back at the Dundee High School when Mother drove her across the ferry to St Andrews on Wednesday 20 September, a few weeks after her thirteenth birthday. This time there were the inevitable tears when mother left, but, as soon as she had gone, they dried. Almost she felt relieved, almost she was glad to exchange the tensions at home for the very different tensions of school.

The dormitory lists were up. She was in 'ten', part of the new section built on to the old stone Victorian house which stood right on the cliffs next door to the ruins of the castle with its famous bottle dungeon. The long room was divided into ten cubicles, five on either side of a passage and were separated from each other by a thin partition with curtains which could be drawn across the front for privacy. As a new girl, she was allotted one of the middle cubicles. She also found out that she was to be fag to a beautiful girl with long red-gold pigtails and a scatter of freckles called Ailsa Craig who was head of the dormitory.

She had been never been so busy in her whole life. There was no time to be homesick. The day started at 7 am with the gong. Half an hour was allotted to wash, dress, plait her hair, roll back the bedclothes to air them and arrive in the dining room for breakfast; porridge or corn flakes and a glass of milk. Twenty minutes later you were back in the dorm to make your bed and tidy your cubicle. Then into the day-room for 'early work' at 8 am. This meant getting your books arranged in the satchel for school work, finishing off bits of undone prep, writing up your diary, or, if you were a fag, tidying your monitor's desk Ailsa complained that her desk was perfectly tidy until Betty rearranged it.

By 8 30 at the latest it was time to put on your galoshes, wrap yourself in your cloak and walk the ten minutes or so (it could be done in seven) through the narrow streets of St Andrews to the main school gates, through the quadrangle and into the Castlecliffe cloakroom where you had your own peg and locker for your galoshes. At 8 45 the school bell clanged to announce it was time to assemble in the hall for morning prayers. Class by class, the girls lined up with their form mistresses at the end of the row to sing a hymn, bow their heads while Miss MacFarlane prayed and listen to one of the sixth formers reading the Bible lesson for the day.

As a new girl, she was right at the front. She was horridly conscious that one of her pigtail ribbons has come off during the scramble. It was inevitably noticed by her housemistress, who, with the other staff, sat behind Miss Macfarlane on the platform. She was duly summoned to 'the passage' at break where all encounters, most of them unpleasant, took place with the staff. 'Your hair is a disgrace,' she was told shortly. 'Go down to the cloakroom and redo it now.'

Hair ribbons, regulation brown, were a trial. Each night they had to be damped and wound round her bed-post to dry without wrinkles. At the beginning of term she had about a dozen spare ribbons in her chest of drawers. No need to worry about losing one of them quite yet. A fellow new girl suggested she tie her hair in one plait which would need only one ribbon. Ailsa Craig, who had similar problems with her glorious mane which was always escaping in little tendrils round her ears and on her brow, suggested using a slide and loaned her one to try. She clipped it over the rubber band at the end of her thick single plait. Though it did nothing to control the untidy wisps that were too short for the plait, she loved that slide. Its heavy tortoiseshell frame anchored her hair neatly down her back and her housemistress's critical examination brought forth a curt approval

That was until her next drill period. Marching round the room, bending and stretching, jumping on the spot were fine, somersaults on the beam, rope climbing, and the horse were not, specially the horse. How did you begin to catch hold of the pommels and swing your body over? It didn't seem possible. The more she knew she couldn't do it the less she was able even to try. Miss McNaught had no sympathy.

'For heaven's sake, just do it,' one of the other girls urged impatiently. So she did.

Lumbering over at great speed she fell heavily on the mat. Meanwhile her pigtail took on a life of its own. It swung round and hit Miss McNaught in the face. Her nose began to bleed. Next holidays she had her hair cut.

Two lesson periods of forty minutes followed prayers before break when the monitors chased you outside so that they could enjoy their cocoa and buns and a good gossip in peace. After three further periods they all returned to the house for lunch. If, as occasionally happened, you had a spare period you went to the library to work.

The library was a detached house adjoining the school grounds which had once belonged to Mary, Queen of Scots. It was a magical place crammed with rickety passages, winding wooden stairs and what seemed like dozens of small rooms each of them devoted to scholarship. The history room, geography, fiction, literature, science and language rooms were wall-papered with books and furnished with plain wooden chairs around a central table for study. Each room had its own characteristic fragrance, a mixture of wood polish, old books and silence. Some of the books you could borrow, many of them were so precious that they could only be read on the spot. Most of the rooms looked out on to an old walled garden. If you stood in the garden and looked up you could see the queen standing at the window of her room, or so it was said. She found it quite by chance, the queen's room. It was small and dominated by a four-poster bed complete with hangings, Queen Mary's bed.

She stood looking down on it willing the ghost to appear. Slipping off her house-shoes she dared herself to lie down on the bed. It was so short! How did the queen manage? She had been six foot tall. Bending her knees up and cradling her head with her hands she thought about the queen. Though she could not see her, she could feel her presence all around. Could, then, the queen see her? If, as father said, you lived on in heaven with God, then perhaps she was looking down on her right now. It was a little scary. She sat up quickly, respectfully, for she knew that the queen was here, present at this moment, standing beside the bed. She did not have to materialise for Betty to know this. She also knew that the queen was not angry for she had a half smile on her face. From that conclusion, Betty learned a little more about death. She even wrote a poem about it. She sent it up to the school Literary Society but the comment that came back was crushing, 'You should not write about something which you have not experienced.' That did not change her mind, however. Peter Wilson, her rector at All Saints, called it the Communion of Saints.

After lunch they had half an hour's free time. The monitors huddled round their desks gossiping while the younger girls scanned the lists to find out where and what they were scheduled to do that afternoon. At 2 pm precisely the housemistress came into the schoolroom. The games captain of the house with the list stood beside her and the rest lined up in a queue. 'Please may I play lacrosse.' 'Please may I be off-play' (a euphemism for having the curse). 'Please may I play fives.' 'Please may I play golf.' Or if the weather was wet, 'please may I go for a walk along the Lade Braes, or the shore, or the cliffs'. Or, and this was truly to be dreaded, 'please may I go for a run.'

She soon learned just how hateful lacrosse could be in spite of the padded gloves, though it was perhaps a degree less hateful than hockey which was played in the foulest of weather throughout the spring term, on a par with summer's cricket which was boring and chilly. Whatever was written on the list had to be done.

She had always known that St Leonards was a 'gamey' establishment. Along with the school hymn (*Through the Night of Doubt and Sorrow*), the school motto, (*Ad vitam, St Leonards,*) which had to be learned by all new girls, there were also team sports which went by the euphemism, 'play'. New girls were watched with keen interest by the monitors as they stampeded up and down the pitches cradling the lacrosse ball or dribbling with a hockey stick. She was immediately marked down as useless. Unfortunately this did not mean that you could get out of trying. Far from it. You were coached by ruthless sixth formers until you at least understood the rudiments of the game.

The alternative was, in fact, worse. A run. Led by a monitor and her partner, you and yours had to keep them in sight at all times. If you lost them, you were either shouted at, shrivelled by sarcasm or reproached for slacking. You were in bad odour with everyone. Tennis was all right. Fives was almost fun once your palms got used to being sore and swollen, but walks with a chosen partner when you discussed life in general and school in particular were best.

After 'play' you bathed and changed into your afternoon dress. These were plain wool frocks of your own choosing. She loved hers which was bright turquoise, much the prettiest she had ever owned until the underarms got stained white with sweat because she had forgotten to sew in the little white moon-shaped pads that protected the material.

After a plain tea of milk, bread and marge with marmite or, if you were lucky, a pot of home-made jam, you scrambled back to school for two more periods, then home again for prayers led by the housemistress with a hymn accompanied by one of the girls who learned piano. She was only asked to do this once. Playing in public reduced her fingers to trembling jelly and the rest of the house to exasperation. Then supper at 7 15, always the best meal of the day, and best of the best was macaroni cheese and chocolate shape. After a short period of yelling the bell went for prep. As a new girl, she stopped work at 8 00 and the Lower Fifths and Fifths silently left the room to go next door for 'drawing room'. The book chosen for reading by the house-mistress was an abridged *David Copperfield*. By 9 pm she was in bed and the bell rang for silence. She soon learned like others to read by torch-light under her quilt. The sixths formers were supposed to undress in silence and all the lights went out at 10 pm.

She was usually sound asleep when the air-raid siren's wail awoke the dormitory. Sleepily she followed the drill that had been carefully explained and rehearsed, got up, put on her pink dressing gown and slippers and wrapped herself in her quilt, and, carrying her pillow, followed Ailsa and the others in an orderly fashion down the back stairs to the basement passage that led to the boot-room. Chattering and giggling the girls lined themselves up against the wall and snuggled up in their eiderdowns against their pillows but there was no thought of sleep.

Someone told a ghost story, sometimes singing was started by one of the mistresses at the far end of the passage, *Frere Jacques* or *Row the Boat* sung as a round. There was always a lot of laughter and the housekeeper whose room was next door to the boot-room made cocoa. Someone inevitably farted and everyone yelled indignantly 'Who pumped?' 'How disgusting!' One of the older girls wore a siren suit like Winston Churchill, a wonderful blue felt all-in-one garment that started a fashion. Next term most of the girls had them.

Depending on whether the all-clear sounded before or after midnight, they had an extra hour in bed. Air-raids therefore were popular. Only one bomb ever fell on St Andrews, and, though a cottage was destroyed, no one was ever hurt. Not like London. Picky, the Latin mistress, had a flat in London. A 2C 50 bomb had fallen right through the roof and landed in her bath. She had just got out. She made a great joke of it but it was not really funny.

In spite of her busy schedule there was still time for Confirmation classes. St Andrews abounded in churches. The three main denominations were well-represented. The Episcopal Church in Scotland, wrongly but inevitably known as the 'English' church, had two buildings, one called St Andrews, large, well-filled, conventional and served coincidentally by the Reverend Mr Andrews. The other, All Saints, was small, ritualistic, misty with incense and was shepherded by father's best friend, Peter Wilson. She was, for a while, its only representative in Castlecliffe. When it came to Confirmation, a dozen or so older girls from the whole school gathered in the hall during one of the afternoon

135

periods for instruction by Mr Andrews. She, being the only one attending All Saints, went to All Saints Rectory where she was given lemonade and biscuits, teased a little and taught the Catechism by Father Peter.

It was all light-hearted, rather jolly and jokey until it came to Confession. Father Peter made the arrangement with her housemistress who informed her that she should go to the church the following Friday at noon. 'I've explained to your form mistress. No need to say anything to anyone. Just be at All Saints on time,' she was told briskly. No one asked her if she wanted to make her Confession, nor did it ever occur to her that it was not compulsory. She took it for granted that this was what happened before Confirmation. She was a little dismayed to learn that from henceforth it would be a regular event during Advent and during Lent.

Father Peter had carefully explained the procedure beforehand and given her a little book with the ritual written out. She was appalled as she read through the form of self-examination. Every one of the twenty-one sins against God, her neighbour and herself was relevant except perhaps the sin of adultery, though come to think of it, maybe that too. She was not sure if the little secret discussions she had with her new friend, Alison, or looking up the best bits in the *Song of Songs*, counted as adultery. Probably, but fancy having to tell Father Peter. Would he tell father? Bad enough gabbling her night prayers, lying, being unkind to her sisters, being rude to mother, and so on, etcetera, infinity, but fancy having to tell! She couldn't do it. But of course she had to go.

Father Peter was waiting for her when she entered the misty church. He was sitting beside a prayer desk wearing a purple stole over his cassock and his eyes were closed. Shaking all over she knelt down and took out her book and the list she had written, but it was so dark in church and her handwriting so spidery that she could hardly read it. Her voice was unrecognisable, all shivery and breathless. His eyes were still shut when she had finished. He said a lot of things which she tried to listen to but her heart was beating so loudly that she hardly heard him. He also told her that she should not mention personal names. 'God knows. I don't need to,' he told her kindly. That was a relief. Then he gave her a little bit of the Bible to read for her penance, took off his stole, kissed it and looked at her for the first time. 'Well done,' he said and winked, just like his old self.

She was confirmed a few weeks later on the 25 February in St Andrews church along with all the other girls and some boys too. She wore her white Speech Day dress, black stockings and her black shoes with the lavatory heels which were already a bit tight for her. She also had a white veil fixed by a rather bossy woman who told her where to sit in the third pew from the front. She would be confirmed after Mr Andrews' girls but before the boys.

She knew the Bishop of St Andrews a little because he was a friend of father's who called him the 'Slate Pencil' because that was what he looked like, tall, thin, bearded and very grey. She never knew his real name. Father was there in his clerical frock coat and mother in her fox fur collar because it was exceedingly cold. They had tea afterwards at the Victoria Café and father gave her a beautiful crucifix to hang over her bed. She got a leather prayer book with the English Hymnal from her godfather and a new Bible with the Apocrypha from her godmother but somehow it was all a bit headachy and she was really glad when it was over. Father Peter suggested she made her first Communion in the holidays at Easter in the cathedral. 'I think your father would like it,' he added, so she did. She and mother drove father down for the early service on Easter Sunday and that was to become the pattern 'now that you're so grown up' as Mrs Burns said to her one Sunday.

But of course she was not grown up, nor did Confession make her a better person as was proved to herself by her sulky behaviour during the holidays, her snappiness with her sisters and her general moodiness.

Chapter Sixteen

Bulls and Rum
After the rigours of Easter, father was exhausted, and, though the specialist was hopeful that he would recover, he was ordered a month's complete rest, so the family returned to Shanwell for the whole of Betty's holiday.

Though father was already depressed because nineteen bombs had been dropped close to his family home in Orkney and blown out most of the windows, he hid his worse fears for the future from the children as best he could. Some days he felt strong enough to do a little pruning of the trees in the New Plantation close to Old Bain's cottage. Other days he went walks with the children though it was clearly an effort and Betty and Bunty did much dawdling by the sides of burns, skimming stones or aiming at targets on the far bank to give him an excuse to rest and catch his breath.

Only once was she seriously worried. They had decided to take a short cut across a field without realising that Jimmy Forrester's prize bull had been put there to segregate it from the cows. They were just over half way across the field when Bunty spotted it. Betty was instantly afraid, like after a nightmare. Instinct told her to run, but father could not run. 'Act naturally,' he said. 'It won't run unless we do'. So she forced herself to slow her pace to his, while inwardly a voice was shrieking, 'Hurry up, hurry up, hurry up!' Bunty, though outwardly calm, was as jittery as Betty, and, fortunately, Baby was not with them. The bull had spotted them. It lumbered slowly across the field, then faster in their direction. The fence was in sight, three lines of taut wire topped by a strand of barbed wire. Easy enough for them to squeeze through the lower strands, but how about father? 'Slowly does it,' father urged but even he was losing his nerve. The bull began to gallop. He was within yards of them as the two girls slipped through the lower strands. They leaned on the wire as father threw his jacket over the barbs. They could hear the creature snort. Betty and Bunty, safely over, were sobbing; father, half over, got the ankle of his woollen sock snagged. Six feet away from them, the bull stopped, stared, as with shaky fingers they tried to unravel father's foot. Then it put its head down and started to crop the grass.

Afterwards Jimmy Forrester laughed at their fears. 'Old Fred? He's as tame as a kitten. All he wanted was a bit of company.' Father made fun of the event with a laugh at himself but it hadn't been funny. A far bigger problem than a lonely old bull awaited him at home.

A letter from the secretary of the cathedral vestry had arrived while he was out firmly but kindly stating that as father was no longer fit for the arduous duties of a provost, he might be wise to retire. It was, on the whole, a thoughtful letter which father realised needed to be written, but it left both him and mother deeply depressed. A few days after Betty had returned to school for the summer term he gave in his resignation to the bishop.

She was not there while the big decisions were being made and her parents only hinted at it in their letters. As to where they would go, mother's brother, Bob, a regular soldier, persuaded them to share Shanwell with Aunt Nell and Jill who were also homeless now that the war was in earnest. Baby's godfather who had no family of his own undertook to pay for her education. No one told Betty until she had left school that her sisters' education in St Andrews depended upon her behaviour. She might not have escaped with Alison at night to prowl round the castle walls or sat with the eccentric Janet, dangling their bare legs over the harbour wall, when they should have been studying.

The summer holidays were in full swing when father preached his last sermon to a packed cathedral. The tears poured freely down his cheeks as he said goodbye to the job and the people he had grown to love and who so obviously loved him. Tears are infectious and she and Bunty's eyes were streaming as were those of many of the congregation. Noses were ostentatiously blown and handkerchiefs pulled out of pockets all round her. Only mother was dry-eyed, beyond tears, her face grey with exhaustion and concern.

A week later, the packing done, the furniture in store, they left the rectory and moved to Shanwell. To her joy she had a new room to herself, the blue room, which had once been the guest room. Jill and Aunt Nell were there to welcome them, but not for long. Although Jill at six was thrilled to have three older cousins to play with her, Aunt Nell hated the remote country life and stayed away with friends in the south for long periods at a time. Uncle Bob, having escaped from Dunkirk, was now in Italy serving under General Montgomery so she was continually anxious as well as lonely in a way that mother and father could only alleviate up to a point.

St Leonards, having approved Betty's behaviour, offered as a great concession to take all three girls for the price of one, so, it was decided that, young though Baby was at nine, she and Bunty should go to St Kays that autumn. It would be difficult to say which of them hated it most, but, like Betty, they grew accustomed to the discipline and the ambience. It did not occur to any of the children that they might have an alternative choice, not even when Betty had to have extra coaching in Latin from the head-teacher of Kinross High School. This was war-time after all.

Annie helped them through the move but had set her heart on becoming a Land Girl, so, encouraged by mother and father who were aware of her restlessness, she joined up. Fortunately she was placed on Jimmy Forrester's farm so they still saw her most days and she spent her spare time helping mother in the house. If Annie had hoped by proximity to reawaken Sam's affections, it was a failure. He was firmly in thrall to his bedridden mother and her chosen successor, which is exactly what Mary became. On old Mrs Forrester's death, she claimed Sam as her common-law husband and thereafter called herself Mrs Forrester.

Annie, disappointed and perhaps secretly regretting that she had given Sam up to look after the children, found herself a pen pal in the army. They began writing to each other and the correspondence was to go on for the duration of the war until he was demobbed. She was sure she was going to marry him, so sure that she had begun to put away items for her trousseau. Every birthday or Christmas, the children gave her little gifts to put in her bottom drawer and squabbled as to who would be bridesmaids. His name was Bert and he was English, which gave him a certain glamour. The first news the children sought on their return for the Christmas holidays was a progress report on Bert.

That term father had his first stroke. When they returned for the Christmas holidays he was more or less permanently confined to his room where a fire blazed and he sat with a rug over his knees. His speech was a little hesitant but the main damage had been to his right arm. As he could no longer write he spent hours in his chair struggling to learn to use his left hand so that he could continue to write weekly letters to his children when they were away at school.

It was, however, a happy Christmas with a lot of laughs. The local rector of the tiny St Paul's Episcopal church which had been so much part of Shanwell life, was a kindly man who had the round pink face of a schoolboy and the (rather plump) body of a man. Who

142

first started to call him 'Dick Bultitude' after the character in a book called *Vice Versa*, where a twelve year-old boy became the father and the father became the son, no one could remember, but she suspected it was father who gave nicknames to everyone. He was a frequent visitor to Shanwell for he brought father the sacrament once a week, pedalling the three miles or so on his bicycle, come rain or shine. Whatever the truth of the matter, Dick Bultitude he became and was to remain for the rest of his ministry in Kinross. He lived with his sister who naturally became Miss Bultitude. The trouble was that no one told Aunt Nell.

That Christmas she decided for the first time to come to church. After the service was over, brother and sister stood beaming in the porch to greet the congregation.

'This is my sister-in-law, Nell,' mother introduced her but failed to give their names, so Aunt Nell assumed wrongly in her rather loud, strongly Canadian accent, 'So good to meet you at last, Mr Bultitude, Miss Bultitude.'

The children vanished round the side of the church, collapsing in helpless laughter. Aunt Nell was indignant when they told her the truth. What the rector and his sister made of the remark no one dared to inquire.

Christmas had started on the first day of the holidays. Betty decided to write a play which would be acted by the others. She would be Gabriel, of course, Bunty was Joseph, Jill was Mary because Baby refused to be a girl so she became first the innkeeper, then the shepherds, and then the Wise Men, all three of them. The story was told from Gabriel's point of view which she thought rather ingenious, and also it gave her most of the lines. It occurred to her that the Star was really Gabriel in disguise, so she made herself a big cardboard star and covered it with silver paper and tinsel and led Baby across the makeshift stage in father's room. It was scheduled for Christmas Day after tea.

On Christmas Eve she had gone round to the Kirkie's cottage to play a game of dominoes with Mr Kirkwood It had been a clear frosty night and every star stood out in three dimensions, each seemed to be different in colour, in size and in light. She stood and gazed up in wonder. Suddenly she felt surrounded by love and angels and God and a feeling of anticipation that was far more than Christmas. Oh yes, in spite of father's illness, in spite of war and petrol rationing and poor Latin results, she was flooded with happiness and confidence and joy. 'I shall remember this moment for the rest of my life,' she thought.

On Christmas night after the play and after supper, father asked her to stay behind to say Evensong with him. It was not the first time she had said his office with him but this was the first time without mother being present. God felt very close when she said prayers with her father. God being close made her want to cry. It was very difficult trying to respond, 'Lord have mercy', when your voice was choked up with tears. Father had tears in his eyes too which made it worse. Somehow they got through it and afterwards she felt more grown-up than ever. It was a sad feeling and for the first time she was not sure she liked being grown-up.

On Boxing Day, mother and the girls were asked to tea with the Bultitudes. There were other people present too and it was a splendid tea with a chocolate Christmas log and thoughtful little gifts for them all. After tea, Dick

144

Bultitude took Bunty and Baby upstairs to the attic to play with his model railway. 'Betty can stay with us. She's far too grown-up to play with trains,' Miss Bultitude said kindly pointing to a footstool in front of the fire. It was hot and boring and lasted forever. No, being grown-up was not what she had expected.

Then she changed her mind again.

Aunt Nell was neat and smart and sophisticated. They were all a little afraid of her because she could put you in your place with just a look. It was well known that she was miserable with Uncle Bob away in the war, so they tended to keep out of her way. Three days a week she helped with a canteen at the big air-force camp at Balado She was a great favourite with the officers, so Annie said. At home the drawing room was her domain which she sometimes shared with Jill. Mother spent most of her time in father's room or in the kitchen while the children lived in the library. The huge billiard table had been removed to give them more space. *Racing Demon* was the favourite game that Christmas and required a lot of floor.

One evening before supper she had reason to ask Aunt Nell's permission for Jill to go with the three older girls on a planned bike ride the next morning. 'Go on, you ask her, ple-ase,' Jill had pleaded so she had knocked on the drawing-room door.

Aunt Nell was in a gracious and expansive mood. In the soft lamp light her face looked very red. She looked at Betty closely. 'How old are you now?' she asked, though she must have known perfectly well. 'In my fourteenth year,' Betty replied trying to make herself sound older than she was.

'Come and sit down,' so Betty had sat on the edge of the sofa facing the blazing fire. 'Are you happy?' she asked

Betty had never thought about it. She just was. She could think of nothing to say. Aunt Nell sighed. 'Your mother keeps you so young. When I was your age – but never mind about that.'

She got up and moved over to the decanter to pour herself a drink. 'It's time you learned to grow up a little. What about a drink?' She looked at Betty and raised her eyebrows. 'Just a very little one, of course. She poured some of the brown liquid into a cut glass tumbler. 'Rum, I'm afraid, all that damned grocer had in stock.'

She added some water to the brown stuff and handed it to Betty. It smelt like the gas mask, of dentist gas, but Betty was floating on air. Here she was sitting with a drink in her hand talking to Aunt Nell, the epitome of sophistication. She took a sip of the loathsome stuff.

Aunt Nell laughed. 'Well done,' she said. 'At least you're not a prude. You don't have to finish it.'

'I like it,' she lied, unwilling for the moment to end. She was to become Aunt Nell's slave for the duration.

'I'll tell you what,' Aunt Nell said. 'You can come and help me with my canteen round. Meet a few boys.'

Her cup was full, but mother was not pleased. 'She's far too young,' she protested.

'Perhaps next holidays, then,' Aunt Nell had said with a shrug.

But next holidays had a different agenda.

Chapter Seventeen

Grief

Although going back to school was no longer the agony it once had been, leaving home that January was particularly hard. Father was so frail and mother so anxious. Within a week she had had a letter from him, four lines painfully, painstakingly written with his left hand. She knew this was particularly hard for him because his handwriting, minute and elegant, had always given everyone so much pleasure, himself included. Now it sprawled, illegible and out of control, across the page. His letters written weekly to all of them made her cry.

Two fixtures had been planned to enliven the dark days of winter. The first was a house-party.

House parties happened on Saturday nights. You invited a guest from one of the other houses and various members of the teaching staff were also asked and 'shown round' by one of the monitors and there was party food on offer. During the war this usually amounted to fatless, eggless, sugarless sponge cake and spam and Stork margarine sandwiches, but welcome nevertheless. She was always hungry.

Entertainment could be anything from a concert pianist to DIY reviews, skits or sketches. That term it was to be a competition, 'Come as a Book Title', with several prizes. The acting chest in the attic was plundered for the best costumes and all the contestants numbered. *Oliver Twist,* at number one, wore a pair of blue pyjama bottoms rolled up to resemble ragged trousers, bare feet and carried the housekeeper's dog's tin plate borrowed for the occasion.

Jane Eyre, at number seven, wore an ingenious bonnet made of white lace and black crepe paper. Four girls from the lower fifth were *Little Women*. *Peter Rabbit* wore a fawn siren suit with a blue bed-jacket and pink crepe paper ears and Helene went as *Alice in Wonderland* with her long fair hair loose and held back by a snood. Alison went as Long John Silver in *Treasure Island* with a black patch over one eye and a cut-out cardboard parrot which refused to sit upright on her shoulder and Betty, at number nineteen, was *Witchwood* in a steeple hat and broomstick. Some of the visitors excelled themselves with costumes borrowed from the acting chests of their various houses. Much the easiest to guess was *Sherlock Holmes*, with pipe, deerstalker and plaid trousers.

Un-guessable, however, was Janet. She appeared in the hall draped in a heavy black cloak from head to foot like an Arab in a burqa. Indeed someone suggested *The Sheik*. People clutching note pads and pencils begged for hints but as her mouth also was covered she would or could not answer. Soon the party was in full swing.

The ring of the outside bell went unheeded for several minutes for the cook and the two remaining ancient maids, who had not been called up, were also watching the fun. Eventually an extremely irate Air-Raid Warden strode into the crowded hall. 'Put out those lights,' he thundered. Did they not realise there was a war on? Perhaps they wanted the whole German air-force to descend on St Andrews? 'What are you thinking of?'

The housemistress somewhat stiffly asked him to explain himself.

'The black-out, madam. Where is your black-out?' he snorted.

148

The schoolroom had an annex attached to the far end where the lower fifth-formers congregated. Not in use this particular evening, no one had noticed that the black-out curtains had gone. Light streamed out into the garden and over the sea.

They looked at each other. When? Why? Who? Someone afterwards confessed that she immediately thought there must be a spy in the school. Then everyone looked at Janet.

'Who are you supposed to be, anyhow?' they all asked.

'*Jude the Obscure*, of course' she told them huffily as she shrugged off the offending curtains.

Of course. Who else? Betty didn't like to admit that she had never head of *Jude the Obscure*.

The other distraction was a one-act comedy called *Marigold*. Girls who were not studying for Lower or Higher School Certificates or university entrance exams shared the twelve parts between them, six male and six female. She was cast as the equerry to the handsome officer hero, a lower sixer, called Rosemary. She had one line of three words to learn, the punch line, which came right at the end of the play and which was supposed to reduce the audience to laughter and applause before the curtains were drawn. One line, three words, that was all, but much was made of its importance. She wore a splendid navy blue uniform with brass buttons down the front and gold chevrons on the sleeve, only a shade less resplendent than Rosemary in a scarlet jacket with gold epaulettes. The women too were splendidly and suitably dressed in bonnets and shawls or mob caps and aprons depending upon their station in life. She sat through numerous rehearsals which seldom reached the end of the play. It was not thought necessary. She muttered her single line over and over again, aloud, in the bath, or to anyone who would listen, but mostly in her head.

The last Saturday in February came all too quickly. One of the other houses had been invited for the occasion and the schoolroom was crowded. Part of the annex was adapted as a stage, and, much excited, the cast dressed up in the housemistress's room next door. Someone had a lipstick which was over-generously shared by all, male parts included. Two lower fifths were in charge of the curtains, the lights went out and the play rollicked towards its conclusion.

She had been growing more and more nervous as the time for her appearance came closer. As the rest of the cast settled confidently into their roles, she began to shake. Suddenly the house-mistress was hissing at her, 'You're on.' Catapulted forward she stood there blinking at the lights. Her throat had seized up. Worse by far, the words had gone. The cast stared at her expectantly, the audience was silent. Then all at once everyone on stage was mouthing the three words at her. She took a deep breath. 'The jeelie's jeeled!' she croaked and the house erupted in laughter.

'Well done,' the housekeeper said kindly when the curtain calls were over. 'I liked the way you made us wait for the punch line.' No one else said anything.

The long winter months stretched into spring. A week before the end of term, the housemistress called her into her room while the rest of the chattering house were pulling on their galoshes and wrapping themselves around in their cloaks for morning school. She told Betty to sit down. She herself stood facing the fire, not looking at her for a moment then she turned and Betty was shocked to see that there were tears in her eyes. 'I have some bad news, I'm afraid.'

It shouldn't have come as a shock. Mother had written earlier in the term to say father had had another slight stroke, but that he was all right. He was not all right. He had died of a third stroke early that morning.

The tears which had never been far away when she thought of father, rose in a great fountain of grief. She thought she would never stop crying. Some part of her must have heard her housemistress telling her what arrangements had been made to get her and her sisters back to Shanwell.... Her sisters. The tears erupted again. Afterwards she heard that Bunty had been made to sit a Latin exam. Miss West had thought it would take her mind off her grief. She was ashamed because she did exceptionally well. Later the three sisters were sent for a walk on their own before the car came.

Mother was dry-eyed, calm. All she told them was that their father had been happy to go but sad to leave them all. Otherwise nothing was said. There was no thought of seeing him. She did not even know where he was. For that, she supposed she was thankful. The least mention, even the thought of her father, triggered the tears. Was it better that way, that Annie and Aunt Nell and their friends at Shanwell should say nothing? That father's name was henceforth left out of all conversation?

As a communicant, she alone of the children was taken to the requiem mass held in little St Paul's. The church was full of clergy who had come long distances because her father had been much loved. Bishop Proudie officiated. When she knelt at the communion rails she could have reached out to touch the coffin. That was the nearest she ever got to seeing him again. She was not taken to the burial in the local churchyard, nor did any of the children visit the grave until the following summer when the granite cross was erected.

As a way of coping with grief, silence was not successful. Far from helping her to grow up, to take her share of responsibility, to be a support to her mother, it turned her into a child again. Her moodiness increased fourfold, she was rude, she quarrelled, she argued constantly with her sisters and she was no help at home. She overheard mother once say to Aunt Nell, 'Betty's become so difficult'. She knew it was true but she didn't know how to change.

At school that summer term she felt diminished, ashamed, unconfident, lost. It was the shame that bothered her most. To have no father, for everyone to know she had no father, destroyed all the self-confidence she had once had. She was ashamed of her shame.

The long summer holidays brought further anxieties. Money was a problem. Mother's church pension was a pound a week. There were few dividends. Baby's godfather was always late with the school fees. The car had to go. Mother was encouraged by her friends to join them in packing parcels for POWs in Perth. Sometimes she went with her and on to the cinema in the afternoon. The cinema became her lifeline. It didn't much matter what the film was, western, romance or war propaganda, she lost herself in the story and for a few hours was, if not exactly happy, no longer itching with discontent and misery The cinema and the radio. *Monday Night at Eight,* the afternoon play, the weekly serial, Valentine

Dyall as *The Man in Black*. Then after everyone else went to bed, she was allowed to take the wireless, accumulator and all, to her room where she listened to music, Glen Miller, Geraldo, Bing Crosby, Ann Sheridan. She began to think about boys. The long steep climb out of grief had begun.

Chapter Eighteen

Boys etc.

The trouble was that there were no boys. The household at Shanwell was all female apart from Mr Kirkwood who was in his seventies and hardly counted as a boy and old Fowlis at the Lodge who might have been a hundred. Though St Andrews was hotching with Poles and a whole air-force of young men were billeted a couple of miles away at Leuchars there were no male masters at St Leonards. Rumours spread that some of the sixth formers went out at night to meet Poles on the shore or behind the hedges in the garden but she saw no evidence of it. That some of the mistresses befriended the Polish officers was undoubtedly true. The art mistress Miss Hodges made no secret of it. She invited the artistic ones to use her studio by the harbour for their own painting and eventually she married one of them.

Miss Hodges also made no secret of the fact that the headmistress had chided her for coming to school in bare legs and sandals. It was considered unseemly. Even the youngest fifth former had to wear socks with house shoes. 'But there's a war on,' Miss Hodges protested and caused further scandal by painting her legs with a seam to resemble stockings and her toe-nails scarlet. She was absent for about a week before the headmistress capitulated in so far as to allow her to wear socks with her sandals.

That summer three Italian POWs were sent to work on the Shanwell farms. They were lively, with knowing black eyes and irresistibly attractive broken English. She would have liked to fall for one of them as some of the farm women had done, but they were tiny, barely came up to her shoulder, not fancy-able by any stretch of the imagination. One of them, called Luigi, converted silver sixpences into rings for half a crown. Annie negotiated the deal for her, and, in due course, she received the dinkiest little ring with an E etched on it. She wore it on her little finger all through the holidays.

That summer Aunt Nell was as good as her word and took her to help with her canteen in Balado. They drove round the various Nissan huts in a little green van where groups of RAF congregated to buy shaving cream, soap, toothpaste or any other small luxury that was on offer. There was banter. Aunt Nell was good at banter, returning wit for wisecrack. Betty's tongue was paralysed with shyness. One lad however detached himself from the queue around Aunt Nell's end of the van to talk to her. He told her his name was Jim and he made her laugh. Suddenly he said, 'Like the pictures?' She did not realise that this was an invitation and started to chat about what she had seen the previous week, something with Don Ameche in it. 'Well then?' he pressed her. 'Six o clock outside the picture house tonight?' He moved away before she could say yea or nay.

She told Aunt Nell who roared with laughter. 'Do you want to go?' she asked. Of course she wanted to go. This was a date, wasn't it? A proper date. She cold hear herself back at school. 'I went on a date,' she would say in a lordly fashion. 'Did he kiss you?' they would ask. Would he? She was not sure she wanted him to kiss her. He had a lot of spots.

There was an almighty row. Mother and Aunt Nell went at it hammer and tongs for most of the afternoon. Mother's claim was that she was far too young. Auntie Nell said it was high time Betty learned to cope with young men. Mother said he was only an airman of the humblest rank. Aunt Nell answered 'what do you expect, he can't be more than eighteen'. In the end they reached a compromise. Aunt Nell rang up his commanding officer, who was a friend, for a reference. He was as amused as she was. In the end it was agreed that Annie would take her by bus into Kinross, and, to her shame, both Aunt Nell and mother were waiting at the bus stop to walk her home. Jim neither held her hand nor offered to kiss her, but he gave her a tiny box of Black Magic chocolates which they both scoffed.

That summer mother took them to Elie for a week's holiday to stay with Cousin Mary at the Castle. Not much bigger than an average house, the castle nevertheless possessed all the proper features, castellated walls, slit windows and one small turret. Its garden, a wind-bruised lawn with a sundial, ended at the sea wall with steps down to the beach.

Once there had been four cousins in the castle; Cousin Isabel who spoke Arabic and was doing hush-hush war work in Egypt, Cousin Martha who wrote children's history books, Cousin Elizabeth who was married and had two or three sons all grown up and known collectively as the Bevan boys and Cousin Mary who had cats and did voluntary work in an Elie canteen for Poles.

'Why don't you go with Poles?' Baby asked mother once, which luckily made her laugh.

She had not been looking forward to Elie. 'It'll be boring,' she yawned to anyone who would listen until Aunt Nell told her sharply that her mother needed a break, and not to make life more difficult for her than it already was.

'Tell Betty to bring her tennis racket,' Cousin Mary had suggested. 'I gather the tennis club is quite lively.'

Huffing and puffing a bit, Betty did as she was told. They arrived off the bus on a Monday in August and hefted their overnight cases, with her Blue Flash racket attached, the short distance to the Castle where Cousin Mary, who, to Betty's reluctant admiration was an excellent cook, had a wonderful tea prepared.

She was given the turret room, which was round, with a low ceiling, a bed, a bookcase and three little slit windows. 'I thought you'd like a room to yourself,' Cousin Mary told her. 'It used to be mine. The books too.'

Already she loved the room. She was not so sure about the books. They all seemed to be rather learned. 'There's one I think you might like,' Cousin Mary said pulling it out of the shelf. 'See what you think.' She put it down on the bedside table. 'Come down when you're ready.'

The book lay there unopened until after a long evening of playing card games - Cousin Mary was a patience addict - and it was well after ten before she escaped to

156

bed. Because she had forgotten to bring her current reading, *Seven for a Secret* (she had become a Mary Webb addict) she picked up Cousin Mary's choice, prepared to be contemptuous. *Peter Abelard* by Helen Waddell. She read it till two in the morning and from that moment he inhabited her dreams. George Arliss had long gone, Grey Owl was fading, but here was Peter Abelard, very much alive, the most romantic adorable man to have ever lived. She became Heloise and Cousin Mary merited a new respect.

Because of this, she graciously agreed to be introduced to the tennis club. Cousin Mary generously paid for a week's membership and left her with the adult in charge who whipped her away to introduce her to the other teenagers, and there were boys, masses of them. 'Thank goodness you're a girl,' the coach said. 'We're one short this week.' There were two blaize courts and within half an hour she was knocking up with three Glasgow girls who were staying in one of the local boarding houses. Fortunately St Leonards had done wonders for her tennis.

Young people were allowed to use the courts in the daytime but not at night which was reserved for adults, so, day after day, immediately after breakfast she rushed up to the courts for a gossip and a game with the other girls who quickly became her bosom friends. Soon she was joining in their banter with the boys, two of whom were local, one in particular, called Rory, she rather fancied. Not that you could tell. He paid no more attention to her than she did to him. He laughed rather loudly in a voice which growled and squeaked intriguingly. She begrudged every moment spent away from her new friends, including the trip to Ruby Bay, where the beach was supposed to be scattered with rubies. She even sneaked up to the courts in the evening to watch the grown-ups on the off-chance that Rory might be there. Mother, who spent a lot of time trailing the beach with Bunty and Baby, thought her very rude, for when she wasn't at the courts she was in her turret room pouring over *Peter Abelard*. She read it through three times in the week and the romantic bits more often than that.

She overheard mother apologising to Cousin Mary who excused her by saying, 'She's just at that age'.

Back at school she boasted about Rory. While others talked about the boys they had met, the parties they had gone to, the letters they received, she paraded Rory and dreamed about Peter Abelard, but it wasn't enough. All that love to give and it was the same for all of them. Sixteen, she thought; was she the only one never to have been kissed? Jenny already had a fiancé.

Poor Jenny. Her brother, only a couple of years older than herself, had joined up. 'He won't be coming back,' she said shockingly. 'He knows it. We all know it'

'How do you know?

It was because of an old prophecy, she explained, if the thorn tree growing on the castle wall where she lived in the Highlands died there would be no heir. 'It died last winter,' she said. She was right. A few days later news came that he had been killed. He had been run over by an army truck before he even reached the battlefield. Jenny left school shortly afterwards. She married at seventeen.

So much love.

'Grand passions', or GPs as they were called, helped to take the place of boyfriends among all those girls whose fathers and brothers and childhood sweethearts were at war, or worse still, 'missing believed dead'. Most of the girls had a GP, either on an older girl or one of the staff. You giggled a lot, did some harmless stalking, fantasised with your best friend on walks or in one of the music rooms. Betty wrote stories for Midge based on the premise 'What if...'

A lot of girls had crushes on Loopy, who was good at games and ended up captain of house. She was a tall shy girl who kept her distance from everyone, a mystery even to her peers, which was perhaps why she had such a large following. 'What if...Loopy asked me to go for a walk?'

Betty had gone through her life buoyed up by her passions. George Arliss, Disraeli, Grey Owl, Peter Abelard.... These were for home. At school her crushes were flesh and blood, though her imagination turned them likewise into phantoms.

The English mistress was succeeded by the housemistress who in turn was succeeded by the art mistress, bare legs and all, in due course to be displaced by one of the two French mistresses and there it remained; the French Literature mistress. She had sunset red hair, hooded eyes and a caustic tongue, a little like Auntie Meg, a lot like a female version of Grey Owl, come to think of it. It started as a challenge. After a particularly harsh lesson she was determined to attract her attention.

Sometimes Betty hated what she had become, a pleaser. She had learned how to turn on the charm, especially how to charm old people (everyone was old over the age of 20). She had tried it on Cousin Mary to great effect, who was fooled. She did it to Aunt Nell, though she knew

Aunt Nell saw right through her. She was what Hannah used to call a 'sook'. At school she knew well how to 'suck up' to authority.

She gave her whole mind to the conquest. Little things like being there to hold open the door for her before a lesson, gazing at her with attentive eyes while she expounded on *Eugenie Grandet* or *Un ne Badine pas avec L'Amour*, (indeed!) working a little harder on her essays, being the first to leap forward to pick up the chalk when she dropped it under her desk. Smiling a lot. Widening her eyes. She watched herself with wry amusement and not a little shame. Flirting, Alison said scornfully. She grew cocky for she knew she was succeeding.

French Grammar was taught by an elderly teacher who was bullied by the younger classes and ignored by the older girls. She had come out of retirement to oblige the school because of the war. The upper school was studying First Aid and the practical exam was that afternoon. Everyone had her First Aid manual propped up on top of her French Grammar book. No one was listening to the lesson. Suddenly the old grey teacher lost her temper. She swore at them, flung her book across the classroom, burst into tears and strode from the room. Even that shameful episode was to further her conquest.

She reported the appalling episode privately to French Literature. What should she do to make amends? French Literature listened to her attentively. 'You must apologise', so she did, gushingly, and, though French Grammar could not help asking where were the others, which she could not answer for she had not spoken to them, a truce was reached. But her goal had been achieved. French Literature commended her.

After the episode with the flowers, it all got out of hand. Most of the older girls shared a garden plot, a narrow strip of ground sheltered from the worst of the east wind by a south-facing wall. Some of these gardens had been long established with annuals planted years before. She and Midge inherited a particularly good plot which rioted in lupins, pink peonies and big white daisies. One Saturday afternoon when they were free, Midge had an idea. 'Why don't we give some flowers to you-know-who?'

So they picked the best, ignoring the lupin petals which were beginning to drop, and took them round to the flat in town which French Literature shared with a university lecturer.

They were accepted, and, as Midge teased her afterwards 'I don't know who blushed the reddest, you or her.' Blushing was all part of the game. For it was a game, a game that was about to go badly wrong.

GPs are not meant to be reciprocated. The image on the pedestal can never be human. When French Literature made an arrangement to see her on her own in one of the small empty classrooms she took her *Racine* and exercise book with her. She was doing French for Higher School Certificate and was pleased at the thought of some extra coaching. They sat down; she took out her book.

But it had nothing to do with French. Afterwards she was not too sure what it had all been about. The words 'emotional relationship' and 'mutual' stood out in her memory. French Literature had also taken her hand which she had kept tightly clenched aware that it was damp with sweat. She had muttered some desperate denials which French Literature seemed not to hear. 'If we were two old ladies no one would pay any attention but people are beginning to talk,' she said

There was a lot more in the same line, then the bell went for break. She got up, kissed her somewhat clumsily on the cheek and left the room knocking over a chair which Betty automatically hastened to pick up. She wanted to laugh hysterically. Instead she sat down stunned, then she went down to the cloakroom and locked herself in one of the lavatories. She watched a cockroach crawling across the floor and disappearing under the door without really noticing it.

She made the fatal mistake of telling Alison who said that unless she reported what had happened to the housemistress, she, Alison, would. So Betty did. The story did not come as a shock or even a surprise. All her house-mistress said was to tell her that when two people loved each another and it was not suitable, they had to stop seeing each other. 'But,' she protested inwardly, 'I don't love her'. Then she thought maybe she did. Maybe I do. Maybe I'm a lesbian.

Midge thought about it. 'Do you want her to kiss you properly?' she asked. Betty's immediate thought was 'Yuck'. Could you love someone and not want them to kiss you? It was to remain a dilemma until she left school.

That winter she went to her first grown-up dance with Aunt Nell at Balado. She wore a dress that had belonged to Aunt Nell that was a little tight and had her hair permed for the occasion. It looked very strange, a bit too dry and frizzy. She wore a lot of lipstick and mother told her it was far too much so they had a row. Mother also made Auntie Nell promise not to let her drink.

Though she loved to dance, especially reels and waltzes, foxtrots and quicksteps were not among her favourites. At school dancing classes, being tall, she had always led as the man. Having a man lead was a new and difficult experience. Aunt Nell saw that she had plenty of partners but they were all so old. One of them held her a bit too tightly and tried to ply her with gins and tonic until Aunt Nell told him she was only sixteen. He backed off, hands held up, apologised and said he had thought her twenty-five. Twenty-five! Was that a compliment? She did not think so. By midnight she was bored and tired and wanted to go home, but Aunt Nell was sitting on a table swinging her legs surrounded by men, laughing and joking and enjoying herself.

Next day she told everyone how much she had enjoyed it. Aunt Nell said she had done very well, made herself really popular which was nice of her. Both were lies and they both knew it, but, loyal to each other, they both kept up the fiction. Betty was almost pleased to be going back to school.

Chapter Nineteen

Grown-Up

A career loomed large on the horizon. Most of her friends were going on to University, Alison and Janet to Oxford, Midge to Bedford Physical Training College, Anne to London University, Tricia to a secretarial college and

June to do nursing at St Thomas'. All she wanted to do was to write poetry and short stories. She knew, however, that she was not good enough at either to make a living. Having sent poems up to *Punch* on a regular basis, (the only magazine Castlecliffe subscribed to) and had them constantly rejected, she had no illusions as to their quality. She never doubted that she would continue to write but she never quite saw herself 'a writer'. There was no school subject she was particularly good at, not even English. She wasted far too much time scribbling that un-publishable poetry. The war was almost at an end so the thought of joining up was discouraged both at school and at home. A career, however, she had to have. Mother could not be expected to support her indefinitely. In those cash-strapped years, there was no such thing as a 'daughter at home', as mother herself had been.

In school, career talks occurred from time to time, but nothing appealed. Then one Sunday afternoon a young priest called Dennis Taylor came to the school to talk about social work. He himself ran a Residential Youth Hostel for the Scottish Episcopal Church and he made it sound as if there was nothing in life more worth-while doing. 'Come and see it for yourself,' he encouraged her afterwards, and, as the hostel was situated only a few miles away from Shanwell, she agreed to visit in the holidays. He also spoke about probation work in prisons, almoners in hospitals, adoption and fostering (the Episcopal Church had its own Adoption Society), the Council of Social Service in Edinburgh. She leaned forward in her chair, her mouth a little open, entranced. By the end of the afternoon she knew exactly what she wanted to do. She would need her Higher School certificate to matriculate, and, on that proviso, was accepted within weeks to study Social Science at Edinburgh University.

Now that Father Peter had left St Andrews to become bishop of Moray, All Saints had a new rector, a burly, curly-headed, jokey, youngish priest called David who had once been one of her father's curates. She often called in at the rectory on her way back from school where he would offer her a surreptitious cigarette and a friendly ear. When she told him about her choice of career, he nodded. 'It's the next best thing, I suppose.'

'Next best?' she asked surprised.

'I imagine with your background you would have been called to the priesthood had you been a man,' he said in the humorous voice he always used with her.

'I don't think so,' she had retorted in the same tone, but when she thought about it, she realised that he was probably right. It was only a joke, however. The idea of woman priests was, in the forties, inconceivable, so she thought no more about it. With some free time now that her subjects were reduced to English, Latin and subsidiary French, she became more part of the congregation. Old ladies who had lived splendid lives long ago asked her out to tea. She played the piano for Sunday school parties, *Musical Bumps* or the *Grand Old Duke of York.* She was thrilled when Miss Bennett, who taught Scripture at St Leonards, asked her to lead a Sunday School class of six little boys in All Saints on Sunday afternoons. Her housemistress thought it an excellent idea. 'It will stand you in good stead for your social work,' she said.

Teaching Sunday school was no sinecure. The small classes, arranged in year groups, were each held in a different part of the church. Her little group aged about six to eight, was clustered round her near the front door, and, right from the word go, the little boys were unmanageable. Though they looked like angels with their pink shiny faces and scrubbed bare knees, they behaved like little devils. All they lacked were pitch-forks and forked tails. One of their tricks was to open and slam the heavy oak door, making the whole church vibrate. Racing each other round the side aisles was another exploit, though this was usually stopped by one of the other teachers whom, for some reason or other, they instantly obeyed. She tried to storify the lesson for the day as brightly as she could but the little boys, aware of her school uniform, saw her as one of themselves and felt no need to pay her any attention. They scribbled on their prayer books, kicked each other's shins and drew rude pictures in their note-books. Miss Bennett came over from time to time to restore a little order but Father David, whom they respected, just laughed. 'Small boys are programmed to disrupt,' he told her but it was no laughing matter.

She came to dread Sunday afternoons, so much so that after three horrible Sundays she developed a headache. Dubs told her to lie down and gave her an aspirin. She also undertook to ring Miss Bennett. The headache became a weekly occurrence. She took her revision to bed and Dubs, who knew exactly what was the matter, made it easy for her. 'I'll tell Mr Borland that you have too much school work at present. I always thought it a bad idea,' she added with a sniff. Dubs was very

166

Presbyterian and did not approve of All Saints which she said was 'next door to Rome'. So there was no more Sunday school.

It was all rather humiliating but at the same time a huge relief.

All the talk among those going on to university was of summer jobs in the long months before term started in October. She and Midge and some half-dozen younger girls decided to stay on at school for a week of the holidays to pick raspberries in the nearby Carse of Gowrie, famous for its fruit. The girls were commended for their loyal support of the war effort, but, in reality, she needed to make a little money. She had seen a cotton dress in one of the St Andrews shops and she wanted it desperately. Fashionably cut in autumn colours it exactly matched a thick brown wooden bracelet Alison had discarded while clearing out her desk. She loved the look of the brown bracelet on her brown arms and the brown and green and yellow summer dress would be a perfect match.

Mother had sympathised but made it plain that if she wanted it she would have to pay for it herself because her cash flow was tighter than ever. Nor could she have it until the following month when the new clothes ration allowance was due, so the shop kindly laid it aside until she had the money and the necessary coupons.

It seemed odd to be waving goodbye to the house and to the house-mistress who left them in the charge of Dubs. An ancient Blue Bird bus picked them up from all the houses at 7 am every morning and they were in the berry-fields with their macks and packets of sandwiches by 8 am, weather permitting. It did: a week of unbroken sunshine followed. Their hands were stained red, their arms and legs grew browner and their hair wilder as they vied with each other for the heaviest count. Payment varied according to the amount of berries available, so that sometimes they were paid a 1d a pound, sometimes 2d. Whatever the rate, the most you could realistically earn in a day was 7/6d. Her average was just over 5/-. How then did the tinks, who were there with their caravans in their dozens, manage as much as 9/- or even 10 bob? One toothless wee woman, whose fingers moved like lightning, showed her. Little stones found their way into their pails to increase the weight. Sometimes, Midge told her, but she didn't believe it, urine.

The best part of berry-picking was the evenings. They were allowed into streets in St Andrews which were banned in term time mainly because of the student residences, the cinema, and, most important of all, the fish and chip shop. The difficulty with all these temptations at hand was to save any money at all. She had to borrow five bob from Midge to pay for the dress, but it was worth it. She spent that summer and the next wearing it until it had faded and shrunk and was ripped at the hem.

The rest of the summer passed in a whirl. Digs in Edinburgh to find, a bank account to set up with an allowance of £50 a year which worked out at a pound a week, the head of Social Studies, a fierce little woman called Miss Milne, to consult, the harvest to help with, exam results to await, the Youth Hostel to visit.

'How grown-up you look!' some of the proper grown-ups said with a sigh. 'You're so grown-up these days,' Miss Bultitude told her after church. 'What does it feel like to be grown up?' Jill asked curiously. She smiled a little smugly.

Two days before she was due to leave for university she took a last walk up the High Planting to the bathing pool. It was late September. The fields had a leggy tired appearance, parachutes of thistledown invaded the windy air. Every little gust brought down a shower of yellowish-green chestnut leaves. Darting from tree to tree she tried to catch one in her left hand - right hand didn't count - as she had done every autumn since she could remember. To catch one brought good luck for a whole year and it was extraordinarily difficult. It was also, this year especially, extraordinarily important. The leaf was there, fluttering towards her clutching fingers, then, at the last moment, a teasing wind would blow it out of reach. Finally she caught one. She pushed it into the pocket of her cardigan and relaxed. She sat down by the bathing pool and suddenly there were tears in her eyes.

'What does it feel like to be grown up?' Jill had persisted. 'You'll find out for yourself one day,' she had replied in a lordly fashion. The truth was that she didn't know the answer. She felt no different.

She pulled out the leaf, smoothed its scalloped fingers out and held its coolness to her cheek. She knew in that moment that she would be chasing autumn leaves with her left hand every October for the rest of her life. She would always be the same. Being grown-up was a big lie. There was no such thing.

She leapt to her feet, tore off her dress and plunged into the pool. It was absolutely freezing. 'Thank you, God!' she shouted at the top of her voice making the roosting rooks scatter as she splashed from one side to the other and leapt up the bank. A minute later and she was pulling on her dress over her wet underwear. It was time to go home. She knew now she was not grown up, that even as she grew older, she would never be 'grown-up' because there was no such thing as 'grown-up'. She would go on just being herself for ever and ever, even if she were to become a wife, a mother, a grandmother, even when she was dead, she would remain that same child inside: a child of God. What a revelation. What a relief.